101

Positive Athletic Traditions: Building Positive Team Legacies

Bruce Eamon Brown

COACHES CHOICE™

ISBN: 1-58518-874-3
Library of Congress Control Number: 2003112975
Cover design: Kerry Hartjen
Text design and diagrams: Jeanne Hamilton
Front cover photo: Courtesy of the University of Notre Dame

Coaches Choice
P.O. Box 1828
Monterey, CA 93942
www.coacheschoice.com

Dedication

To the spirit of past warriors.

Acknowledgments

Thank you to all the creative coaches, past and present, who have contributed positive traditions to the culture of sport.

Contents

Introduction

Why Write This Book?

Traditions are part of a coach's legacy. Many times, an individual's memories of athletics are left to chance, based on winning or losing. This book provides some meaningful methods for bringing your teams together and creating positive lessons that can be passed on year to year. As I travel the country and talk to student/athletes, one of the questions that I frequently ask upperclassmen is, "What is your most vivid memory of a senior when you were a freshman?" Too often, it is a memory about the senior who threatened to shave their head, tie them to the goal posts, or "turn them into a mummy" etc. Why does hazing exist? From the kids' perspective, it is simple, they think, "this is what was done to me; and now it is my turn and my right to do it to someone else." This attitude has to change. Coaches need to lead the way by providing an alternative path. A many great ways exist to welcome people onto your team, and create good and lasting memories on a daily basis. Correctly building positive traditions will culminate in the development of seniors who understand and model real leadership and will help instill in those individuals who graduate from your program the good kind of pride (i.e., the shared joy of the inner circle) known as TEAM.

Helpful Hints for Understanding and Applying the Traditions

The traditions are divided into chapters based upon the time of season, people (seniors, community and alumni), and themes or slogans. Before a basic overview of each tradition, a sub-section titled, "lessons from this tradition" is included. The lesson listed is designed to provide you with some insight into the direction you might want to take with regard to each specific tradition and, hopefully, some understanding into the memory that this particular tradition will tend to create for the athletes. It would be a good idea to explain the lesson(s) when introducing the tradition to the team. After traditions are begun, it is also wise to occasionally ask the athletes (especially the seniors) what they have learned from this particular tradition. After the traditions are fully established, allow the seniors in positions of leadership to develop a feeling of ownership by introducing the traditions at the first of the season and explaining the purpose behind them to the younger members of the team.

Tradition Never Graduates

Traditions help shape and reflect the character of your team – past, present, and future. Traditions refocus you and give you perspective, rekindle the spirit of the past, remind you of what is important, and create a link that binds the past to the present. They establish your own history, provide a legacy for future teams, motivate people to a standard of excellence, bond communities, and create positive memories. Traditions are a way of saying, "thanks". They make it easier to remain positive. They can turn work into fun, to a point where helping the coach, the team, the school, and community becomes a privilege. Traditions may be simple things a coach consistently does without even thinking, or they may be complex projects requiring time and extra effort. Either way, positive traditions give life to the collective athletic experience and help sustain a program's successes. You are encouraged to use the profession of coaching and the power of positive traditions to create great experiences, change lives, and build individuals, teams, and communities of character.

Including Positive Traditions in the Core Covenants of Your Team

Having Core Covenants should become one of your team's traditions. Establishing traditions that reflect your Core Covenants will help bring stability and enjoyment to your team, program, and athletes. Covenants are the guiding principles of your program. They are what you stand for, what you are and will be known for, and your team's true identity. A covenant carries much more significance than a promise or a mission. It is a binding agreement where action will be physically visible. If you have successfully identified and taught your Core Covenants, the actions of your team should look exactly like your beliefs. Covenants emanate love and respect, and observers will be able to identify and witness the difference. When Covenants are strong, taught well, and adhered to, they often form a bond where people are permanently bound together in a significant, powerful and positive manner. The coach and the leaders of the team must identify and voluntarily commit themselves to what they want to stand for, and provide a distinctly clear vision for the other potential team members.

What Are Your Core Covenants?

What does your team stand for? What behaviors and actions can you guarantee? What are your "for sures"? The level of commitment of the team members to the Core Covenants will determine the strength of your team. In order to begin, coaches must identify what they want their team to stand for, articulate it clearly, teach team members what it means and exactly what it looks like, and provide a clear vision of it. The next step is to get voluntary commitment from as many team members as possible and work to increase the size of the committed "inner circle". All that is required to become part of the team's "inner circle" is for individuals to understand what the team stands for and commit themselves—in word and action—to those principles. After your inner circle of committed players is established, leaders need to compare their actions with their beliefs, and institutionalize their Core Covenants so that these covenants have a meaningful impact on who they become as a team. Some examples of Core Covenants include: work habits—preparation; a team-first attitude;

respect; discipline; and traditions. The words by themselves are not enough to carry them into behaviors. Leaders need to define, teach, practice, and demonstrate each of their Core Covenants so each team member knows what he is committing to and can turn it into identifiable action.

Positive or Negative Traditions?

The issue is not whether your program will have traditions, but rather will these traditions be negative (hazing) or positive. In that regard, will your traditions produce successful teams, great memories, and lasting friendships? Which path your program chooses is your responsibility as the coach.

You are encouraged to use the ideas presented in this book, along with your own creativity, to adjust the traditions to your age group, sport, and personality and then to begin establishing positive traditions for your program.

1

Traditions to Welcome New Team Members

How players are treated as freshmen will have a great impact on how they treat others when they become leaders. As coach/educators and people most in a position of influence with the young people in their care, coaches need to provide alternative paths to how their programs welcome new team members. Above all, negative practices—such as hazing—must be avoided. More and more of the country's most successful teams have chosen to follow the positive path. They understand that no matter how tame it might appear or actually be, hazing causes damage to people and teams. As such it will never be as effective in making new team members feel welcome as establishing positive traditions. Too often in the past, hazing was the standard form of welcoming new team members—a counterproductive practice that has been (all too frequently) passed on to future generations of athletes and teams. Fortunately, an increasing emphasis exists within the athletic community on developing and sustaining positive athletic traditions. Everyone associated with an athletic program—currently and in the future—will surely benefit from such an emphasis.

Tradition #1—Connect a Senior with a Freshman

❑ *Lessons from this tradition*: Welcome to the team; you have a friend in the senior class you can call on if you need anything.

In the spring when players are about to begin their senior year, have them go to feeder schools and meet with the student/athletes who are going to enter your program for the first time. Going to the feeder school involves meeting these future players on their turf and should provide a level of comfort. Have your seniors describe what the new players can expect as they enter your school and become part of your team. Be sure to leave plenty of time for the younger players to ask questions. Prepare your seniors to be ready to dispel rumors and provide answers for what they believe may be potential problems (real or perceived) and potential benefits. Attempt to have your seniors connect with them in such a way that they are confident that they will be "safe" emotionally and physically.

The seniors need to learn the names of the future players and be prepared to call them by name each time they see them. Team up your seniors with one or a group of players and arrange the next meeting to be on your campus, with the senior showing the younger player(s) around. This personal connection may be all that is needed to provide confidence in each young player to become part of the team and also to start the school year with a positive attitude.

Arrange another meeting right before school begins in the fall, so the seniors can see the freshmen's schedules, and help them find their classrooms. If possible, have them help with any areas where there may be the most concern. Encourage your seniors to intentionally meet the freshmen at least once a day during the first week of school. The seniors should call them by name in the halls, at lunch, in the locker room, and at practice. By alleviating areas of concern, having a senior friend to help show the way and making the connection at the school, your new team members will feel much more welcome and part of the team.

Tradition #2—Senior–Freshman Welcome Picnic

❑ *Lessons from this tradition*: Welcome to the team; this is what we stand for and what you need to do in order to become part of us.

Design and incorporate a senior-freshman get together during the summer. This meeting should also be open to any newcomers or transfers. The nature of the meeting can range from being part of a more extensive retreat or being as simple as a picnic for a couple of hours. Among the purposes of the meeting should be to help establish relationships and help prepare new student/athletes for the transition from the feeder program to your program. Above all, however, the meeting should provide the stage to teach the Core Covenants of your program (refer to the introduction of this book). Your Core Covenants are what you stand for, your guiding principles, and your expectations of each member of the program. They say "here is who we are and here is what we stand for, and by voluntarily committing to them, you can become part of our team's inner circle." Players new to your program should leave the meeting with an extremely clear vision of what this team represents and what it will take for each of them, as individuals, to become a contributing member.

Seniors and coaches need to meet prior to the get together so that seniors can take a lead role in presenting a clear vision of your Core Covenants. The leadership goals for the seniors should include:

- Be an action model of the Core Covenants. In the best programs, if you want to see the history of the program, all you have to do is watch the seniors to see what the team stands for.

- See how quickly they can get the freshmen to buy in to the Core Covenants and to become part of the team's positive traditions.

- Be able to see the Core Covenants in the new players' actions and reward them for their actions.

- Begin building the inner circle by identifying those individuals who have made a commitment to the Core Covenants with their words and actions and those who have not. One of the best things about focusing on commitment is that it weeds out the uncommitted.

- Do not give up on those individuals who do not immediately commit; rather, devise a plan on how leadership can bring them into the circle as soon as possible.

- Give wholehearted support to a policy where coaches demonstrate their commitment to the importance of the Core Covenants by giving the bulk of the playing time to those players who have demonstrated their commitment to the Core Covenants.

- Develop a system for incorporating transfers into the team's inner circle. It is essential that a team's leaders be the first to reach out to those new students. Unfortunately, the first young people to reach out to new students are frequently not the ones you would choose for your children. These students are often the individuals in need of friends or validation for their own personal poor choices they have made (i.e., the more people who can be encouraged to buy into a particular decision or action, the more my own bad choices are validated). More often than not, the last people who usually reach out to new students are individuals who already have a good circle of friends, who make good decisions, and who do not need personal validation. That situation needs to be changed. Most adolescents in a new situation are not comfortable or confident enough to try to work their way into an established group. They are just hoping to fit in somewhere. As such, they will often take the first opportunity presented to become part of the group. Even those students who have a history of poor behavioral choices may just be looking for a chance to change their direction. Your team can and should provide that opportunity.

Tradition #3—Senior-Freshman Feast

❏ *Lessons from this tradition*: Welcome to the team. As leaders in this program, we are glad to have you as new members with us. When you become one of the leaders of this team, you will also become a person who serves others.

Before the start of school, set a date for a meal with the whole team. The coaches and seniors cook, serve, and clean up for a meal for the freshmen, sophomores and juniors. Players being served sit by position played—not by class. If you are on a team that doesn't have positions, a person from each class should be situated at each table. This tradition offers a great opportunity to have your seniors teach and model the manners with which your team eats when it is together either on the road or at home.

2

Pre-season Traditions

Tradtition #4—Tradition of Sacrifice*
(*Submitted by Greg Oldham, head coach; Coupeville High School; Coupeville, WA)

❑ *Lessons from this tradition*: Sacrifice for the team.

Every coach and player in our program gives something up for the season. They chose something that is an "extra" and will remind them of the sacrifices necessary in order to reach excellence. Typically I give up chocolate and one other food item, like pizza. This has become so ingrained that I don't even have to tell the freshmen anymore; they know about it and plan beforehand what they will give up. Whenever they have a craving for that item, they are encouraged to have a positive thought for a teammate.

Tradition #5—Retreats

❑ *Lessons from this tradition*: Togetherness. Interdependence. Fun. Leadership.

Retreats are a positive and popular method of starting a season and building a team. Many thoughts exist concerning what can be expected and accomplished by holding retreats with your team. Depending upon who is involved in the retreat, the retreat can be structured to focus on a variety of objectives and factors, including the following:

Coaches and captains retreat or just leaders and seniors retreat:

- Develop a leadership packet.
- Assess the leadership style of the leaders/seniors in attendance.
- Identify the exact role of the captain(s).
- Remind the leaders that all eyes are on them; it is their responsibility to understand and model the Core Covenants.
- Reinforce the importance of valuing *all* roles.

- Learn when to speak and when to listen.
- Learn the essential qualities of being an athlete in the program.
- Identify the best contribution each individual can make as a leader to this team.
- Identify leadership qualities of other people in each individual leader's life.
- Detail the expectations that the coach has of the captain (and vice-versa).
- Specify the roles and responsibilities of each leader on the team.
- Use the retreat as a process for addressing problems and concerns that the team has.
- Identify potential problem areas.
- Help establish the Core Covenants of the team.
- Identify the traditions the team wants to continue and the traditions they want to initiate.
- What each individual wants his legacy as a captain (or a senior) to be.
- Have the team's leaders create a 30-second video that shows what the team stands for. Limiting the video to approximately thirty seconds forces them to be clear, specific, and succinct.
- Let the leaders help make the team's training rules.

Retreat with the whole team:

- Conduct the retreat with the following rule—no electrical devices and no phones. If a person wants to talk to someone, have him do it person-to-person.
- Have players make a list of their personal assets and liabilities. Accentuate the positive and eliminate the negative. Build on good points and develop an improvement plan that addresses each player's weaknesses.
- Have the team put together a huge jigsaw puzzle. Give each player a piece or some pieces of the puzzle and have them help put the puzzle together on the retreat.
- Develop, define, and set the vision of the team's Core Covenants.
- Identify what each person is committed to.
- Have each individual make an oral and written commitment to the Core Covenants.
- Reinforce the power of believing—believe in themselves, believe in others.
- Eliminate negative people who are going to challenge the Core Covenants.
- Have each player identify where he sees himself in 10 years.
- Ask each player what his biggest gift to the team is.

- Ask each player what the team's biggest gift to him is.

- Name the five hardest workers.

- Name the five players on the team who have the most positive attitudes.

- Name the "must-win plays" that have to be successful for the team to win.

- Name the five most important actions that players must undertake for the team to be successful.

- Reinforce the essential nature of three key preseason questions once asked by renowned football coach Lou Holtz. *"Can I trust you?; are you committed to excellence?; do you care about others?"*

Hideaway retreat:

- Include anyone in the retreat who is directly related to program (coaches, managers, trainers, booster club president, athletic director, etc.).

- Get away so the group can completely focus on the entire season.

- Clarify everyone's role.

- List 10 things that can be or are problems that affect the team; solve them before the season begins.

Tradition #6—Links of a Chain

❑ *Lessons from this tradition*: Visible sign of unity. Interdependence.

Buy a chain and demonstrate the strength of the chain when the various parts of the chain are linked together. Take each link of the chain apart and give one link to every player. On the day of the game or at the end of the season, link the parts of the chain back up to show the strength of the chain. At the conclusion of the season, have each player keep the link given to him before the season started.

Another method of using the chain to help create unity on the team is to present a link to each player who has demonstrated commitment. The decision concerning whom to give the various links can be made by the coaches and the team's leaders. The significance of the individual links may be acceptance by players of their roles and their importance to the overall strength of the chain. Chains are joined links, and one weak spot could cause the whole chain to break.

You may chose to give the first links to the seniors or to those individuals who worked the hardest in the off season. In order to enhance their impact, you can initially give the first links in a public display in front of the team. Subsequently, you can hand the links out in a more private manner, by just keeping some in your pocket and awarding them on the spot to deserving individuals.

The concept that you want to reinforce is that until everyone has a link, you will never be a team. Adopt a policy where your captains are able to give links out, along with your coaches. Your seniors can be the individuals who are designated as the players to give a link to the freshman, signifying the freshmen's acceptance onto the team. Coaches should have their own links, also signifying commitment. An individual link and a united chain are like a ring; it never ends, and represents endless love and commitment to the team. You will find that many of your players will have their link for years after they are finished playing. At the end of a championship season, the team can link their chain onto the chains of other championship teams from the past, adding to the legacy of the program.

Tradition #7—Fast Forward to the End of the Season

❑ *Lessons from this tradition*: Visualizing the finished product. Fun.

Have the players fast forward mentally to the end of the season and identify what they would do to celebrate the final game. Then rehearse how they are going to celebrate. For example, practice cutting down the nets; identify the order of players cutting down the net, how each player gets up and down the ladder, how much of each net each player cuts, etc.

Tradition #8—Mr. Wilson Ball*
(* Submitted by Deb Thompson, head softball coach;
Spring Arbor University, Spring Arbor, MI)

❑ *Lessons from this tradition*: Fun.

Each player takes a softball and decorates it as a person, similar to the Tom Hanks' movie "Castaway." In a figurative sense, each player has their own personal fan club. The softball lives with them for the season, goes with them on every trip, and sits in the dugout.

Tradition #9—Signing the Magna Carta

❑ *Lessons from this tradition*: Commitment to the team and its beliefs. Identify and reinforce the value of a person's signature.

Take your team's "athletic pledge" or list of Core Covenants, write them on a large piece of paper with room at the bottom for signatures, and have a signing party. Frame the signed paper and post it in a place where the players will see it everyday. Before the signing party, give each player their own personal copy and let them take it home and discuss it with family and teammates to decide if they can truly and completely commit.

The following is an example of a player's pledge that University of Oregon football coach Mike Bellotti uses in his program: *"I promise to play the game with great courage and never make excuses. I will play with great intensity and give everything I have. I will finish plays and never give up. I will take responsibility for my actions and inactions. I will continue to push my teammates and myself to be the best in athletics, academics, and in life. I will support my teammates and treat them like family. I will enjoy myself and make football fun for everyone."*

Tradition #10—Take the Field in Darkness—Leave in the Light

❑ *Lessons from this tradition*: Unity. Fun. Excitement to start the season.

For your first practice, have your players take the field in the dark. They enter one class at a time. Once every class is in the middle of the field, they meet and set goals, and commit to the Core Covenants of the team. On the captain's signal that they have concluded the process of identifying their goals, the lights come on, and the team leaves the field together. They then move to a place off the field to meet the coaches, parents, and former players to participate in a social event, such as a barbecue.

Tradition #11—Use Your Game Program to Build a History

❑ *Lessons from this tradition*: Build a history of past success. Link with the community.

In your game program, list every person who has ever been a captain of or an inspirational player on your teams. If possible, identify where they are now and what they have accomplished in their life. In addition, put pictures of every championship team to ever come out of the school in a prominent, highly visible place. Build a history of successful people and teams.

Tradition #12—The Little Man of Self Doubt

❑ *Lessons from this tradition*: Fun. Ability to laugh at yourself. Eliminate negative thoughts and increase positive self-talk.

Everyone has days where they let self doubt or negative thinking creep into their heads. In those instances, they hear the voice of the "little man of doubt". Explain this concept to your players and talk about how to overcome negative thinking. Purchase a "little man" (a doll) and hang him in the locker room, and every time a little doubt creeps in, players need to feel free to talk, punch or stick pins in the "little man." Remind your players not to listen to the negative voice of little men who want to discourage them.

Tradition #13—Game Ball Giveaway

❑ *Lessons from this tradition*: Emotion. Perspective on why an individual plays. Doing something for others. Thanking others for what they have done in a person's life. Get players to think about someone other than themselves.

This tradition can be used to dedicate a season or a key game to someone important in your life. Purchase a game ball for every player, and have each individual autograph their ball and take it to someone to whom the player dedicates the season or the game. Have the player explain what the ball means and express why that person was chosen. Such an action can really be an expression of love for the person, the team, and the season.

Tradition #14—The Blue (or School Color) Dot Club

❑ *Lessons from this tradition*: Fun. Unity. Rewarding effort and work habits. Reminder of goals set.

Buy a roll of blue (school color) tape and use a hole punch to punch out hundreds of blue dots. Keep some of the blue dots with you at all times, and anytime you see a player do something above and beyond normal expectation, award them a blue dot. Encourage players to place the first blue dot they receive in a place where they constantly see it. On the face of their watch or in their wallet are two good places for the first dot. The dot should be construed as a reward and a reminder of meeting personal and team goals, of the one heartbeat of the team, and of the Core Covenants of the team. You can change colors as the season goes along or have different colors for different accomplishments.

3

Senior Traditions

Being a senior in great programs is a special time. On one hand, it may mean more attention, but it also involves more responsibility. In most programs, the privilege of being a senior means doing less and putting responsibilities on the younger classes (e.g., the freshmen carry the equipment bags). In fact, however, helping with duties that are essential for the team, such as physically assisting a coach by picking up equipment, should not be considered punishment. Helping out should be an honor reserved for those individuals who have the most invested. Being a senior should reflect an attitude of "this is our time to lead and serve"; rather than "this is our time to be served." Helping the coach should be a privilege. Find a way to turn the old concept around and make the senior year, the year of complete investment, privilege, and fun.

One of the key elements in a group of people who want to become a team is the positive example of commendable work habits that are demonstrated by your team's leaders and your most talented players. You will *never* see a great team where the leaders and the most talented players are not the best workers. These teams may win some games, even a championship, but they will not be a team, if the most visible members do not model commitment to the Core Covenant of hard work. One of the key attributes of being a senior involves, being the best example of what your program stands for. If your seniors are lazy or inattentive, every underclassman looks at them and is confronted by the thought, "I can't wait to be a senior in this program, look they get to come late, coast through practice, and still start." The exact opposite, however, is true in programs with a strong tradition of senior leadership. The underclassmen look at the seniors and say, "I can't wait to be a senior in this program and play for coach; they are the hardest workers, the front line achievers, the best listeners, and the ones who have the most responsibilities. That is going to be great." In the latter instances, the tradition of being a senior who is a servant leader passes to the next generation of athletes.

Tradition #15—Senior Duty—Give Back

❑ *Lessons from this tradition*: Leaders serve. With age comes responsibility. Give back to the program.

Use your seniors to help with game management at frosh/sophomore games. Seniors should willingly volunteer to perform game-day duties such as serve on the chain crew, keep score, prepare the game site, work the scoreboard, etc. Being a senior does not mean you are above helping and working for others. Being a senior involves willingly giving extra effort and time back to the program and to the future players.

Tradition #16—Master of the Shed

❑ *Lessons from this tradition*: This is our program and our equipment, and we take pride in it. While all players are responsible for their roles on the team, seniors are the most responsible. Turn work into fun. Having fun is being responsible.

One of the highest honors in the program is being named "The Master of the Shed" when you are a senior. This senior controls the cleanliness of the equipment shed. He has complete control of this area, and his word is law. His name is on the door under the sign that says "Master of the Shed", along with the particular year of his reign. He may have an easy chair to rest in after the work is completed, sitting on the deck and enjoying the view. He directs both the distribution of the equipment at the beginning of the practice and where teammates place everything at the end of the day. No one has a higher authority within the walls of the shed. This title can be assigned by the coach, applied for by players at the end of the junior season, or "willed" by the current "Master" to a deserving junior. The names of all past Masters are listed in a dignified manner on the wall. The equipment shed carries the name of the finest "Master" in the history of the program (who can be replaced by the current Master on a vote of the coaches or by a special designee, such as the school's custodian). The Master of the Shed can pay a special tribute to any senior who has done an outstanding job on his assigned duties by adding his name to another list called the Distinguished Order of the Shed – The Masters List. Another possible honor would be to allow the player in charge of specific equipment to sign that particular piece of equipment on the last practice. For example, in this instance, a team's shovels or rakes could be autographed by the player. An award can be established for the post-season banquet.

Tradition #17—Field Prep

❑ *Lessons from this tradition*: The work required to practice or play a game is everyone's responsibility. We take care of ourselves and take pride in our facilities. Helping the team by working is a privilege. Helping the coach is an honor and privilege, not a punishment. The longer you are in the program, the more you *get* to invest.

Every player shares in the responsibility for getting the field or equipment ready for practice or for a game. Seniors have the most or highest responsibilities. They should not sit back and watch the younger players serve them, but rather be the individuals who do the most work. Subsequently, the "senior jobs" become the most coveted. The graduating senior can "will" his job to an underclassman who has shown promise of being a great worker or leader. The senior gets to teach how the job needs to be done to the next in player in line so jobs are passed down from generation to generation. An "all field prep team" can be kept and awarded. An award can be named after the player who ever did a particular job the best.

Tradition #18—Senior Leaders—Team Decision Makers

❑ *Lessons from this tradition*: The older you get, the more responsibility you must assume. Be a decision-maker and base your decisions on what is best for the team, not for you individually. Your voice is important to the team.

Develop a senior leadership team and allow them to be involved in every major team decision. Give them a voice that is listened to in a meaningful way. This group may be every senior, or a group of seniors who are either elected by their peers or appointed by the coaches.

Tradition #19—Informal Senior Night within the Team*
(* Submitted by Greg Oldham, head girl's basketball coach;
Coupeville High School; Coupeville, WA)

❑ *Lessons from this tradition*: Saying thanks to people who have been important in your life and season.

Our seniors are our hardest workers and are loved by the underclassmen because they are so giving. This love shows on our informal "Senior Night" (normally scheduled two nights before our last home game when we honor our seniors). The underclassmen in our program take the time at the end of one practice to tell each senior what she has meant to them. Although we don't have an incredible class of graduating players every year, every graduating class adds to our team's legacy of class and excellence.

4

Traditions for Captains

Tradition #20—All Seniors as Leaders

❑ *Lessons from this tradition*: Every senior who has voluntarily committed to the Core Covenants of the program and has been invested can lead. If you invest, your turn for leadership will happen. The senior year is special. Seniors are what our program is about. Leadership can be a shared commodity. Everyone can be a leader in their own way.

Allow every senior who wants to become part of the leadership team apply. The only requirements are that the individual must have personally committed to the Core Covenants of the team. If you are trying to increase the number of players who compete all four years in the program, open up the leadership positions only to players who have been in the program that long.

Tradition #21—Apply for Positions of Leadership

❑ *Lessons from this tradition*: Voluntary commitment. Lots of leadership needs exist on a team, and they can be shared.

Make a list of every leadership responsibility for your program and develop an exact job description. Post the "job listings" and allow team members to apply for jobs for which they would like to be responsible.

Tradition #22—Team Council

❑ *Lessons from this tradition*: Shared responsibility. The team leadership can influence the team by being involved in all major decisions.

Select your leadership team and have them meet once a week all year long for lunch with you. Choose one topic per week to discuss. The topics can come from the coaching staff, from the leadership team, or from the rest of the team through the leaders. Among the types of topics that could be addressed in these meetings are the following: dealing with the media, helping different players in or out of practice, defining players' roles in school assemblies, the lunch room, etc.

5

Practice Traditions

What will your players remember most about practice? Will their memories be of the more negative aspects of practice, such as the punishments, the boredom, the repetition, the lectures, the reaction of others to their mistakes? Or will they remember the dedication, the fun, the perseverance, the loyalty, and the life lessons?

Tradition #23—Positive Conditioning*

❑ *Lessons from this tradition*: Having fun is working hard. Being good is a privilege. Not wanting to let your teammates down is the most powerful motivator on great teams. Stop having coaches or players associating conditioning with punishment.

One of the most vivid memories an athlete will have about practice will be conditioning. As such, coaches are encouraged to stop using conditioning as a punishment and turn it into a positive tradition and a team-building experience.

If coaches had a choice of being thought of as "positive" or "negative," the vast majority of individuals in the coaching profession would undoubtedly choose being "positive." Most coaches realize that, all factors considered, being positive gets better results. They are aware of the fact that considerable research has shown that being positive is the best approach to reinforcement and skill development (teaching).

Many methods exist for developing team feeling—some are contrived, while others are sincere and believable. This tradition is a proven method for bringing teams together in a sincere, believable way. It also is a method to turn what some coaches consider to be the "worst," or at least the most negative, part of practice (conditioning) into one of the best. In that regard, adopting this tradition can be a positive change both for the coaches and for the players.

---

*Note: This topic is also addressed in the book by Bruce Brown, *Teaching Character Through Sport*; Monterey, CA: Coaches Choice; 2003; pp 101-115.

Developing an Appreciation for Positive Conditioning

Early and throughout my coaching career, I went to watch other coaches work. One of the best opportunities for coaches to improve professionally is to identify who the best coaches are in their area and go observe them in practice. What sport or age they coach is not as important as their ability to teach. In reality there are all types of coaches. One of the unique features of the coaching profession is that it allows for so much autonomy. You will find that there are as many different successful styles of coaching as there are different personalities.

One of the primary reasons that I visited so many schools when I was coaching was an attempt to see for myself why certain coaches are "great." Why are they able to consistently field competitive teams? Why do their players love them? How do they consistently get their teams' best effort? How do they demand and receive appropriate behavior?

Among the factors that I observed and learned from my visits were:

- Go observe practice sessions. Don't evaluate a coach by watching his teams play a game. It is too easy to get caught up in comparison of athletes or the outcome of the game.

- Try to attend practices on a series of days. While you may see many things in the first few minutes, watch for a few days and many other lessons will become apparent. Don't make judgments based on one practice.

- Go observe a different program for a week every year.

- Watch and listen closely to see how the coaches you observe go about building their teams.

- Watch and listen to see how these coaches interact and develop relationships with their players. Relationships are the most critical part of a coach's job.

- Observe how athletes react to their coaches in times of praise and in times of correction.

The following examples illustrate some of the best techniques that I learned during my coaching career about building a team (from both personal experience and observation):

- You build a good team when good leadership exists. The leadership of the coach determines everything. In every instance where there was great leadership, there was a good team.

- You build a good team when coaches understand how to achieve a balanced combination of fun and discipline. All "fun" is generally unproductive time, while all "discipline" is not much different than forced labor.

- You build a team when the group attains tough goals, faces tough challenges together, and has common bonds. That is how team toughness and determination are formed. The best way to describe coaches who can consistently reach this level is someone who is both positive and demanding. A positive-demanding coach gets teams to work hard and set and reach attainable goals. He also finds a way to get his players to enjoy the experience.

- You build good teams when mutual respect exists between the players and the coach. When a feeling of interdependence is present within the group, an attitude that the team is more important than any individual also exists. These coaches usually rely on their own discretion and are not boxed in by too many rules. Rules can get in the way of effective leadership.

Conditioning

When observing other coaches, I saw many successful methods of building teams, each of which helped me formulate my coaching philosophy. On the other hand, I still struggled with how I was doing the conditioning phase of practice.

When you think back to your own memories of conditioning as an athlete, what do you recall? Examples of the types of responses that coaches commonly offer with regard to this question include:

- "It was hard, difficult, unpleasant."
- "We ran when someone on the team fouled up" (we all paid).
- "We ran more if someone didn't finish in a certain time."
- "We ran when the coach was mad."
- "We remember hating the coach."
- "Trying to avoid killing yourself."
- "As long as I wasn't last, I wouldn't be noticed."
- "We ran harder if it was measured or when we were being watched."
- "We remembered that certain days of the week were always hard conditioning days and we tried to coast through practice to have something left."

None of these memories reflect an approach that is either pleasant or beneficial for building a team. In my coaching career, I learned the following about conditioning from observing other coaches (some good, some bad):

- A lot of "positive coaches" go easy on the conditioning because they don't want to be perceived as an "ogre" to their players. Therefore, their teams don't do as much conditioning as necessary and are not in as good of shape as some of their opponents.

- As much as possible, well-organized coaches achieve their conditioning goals by the pace of their practices.

- One effective method of conditioning involves breaking up the conditioning periods throughout practice, instead of doing it all at the end of the practice session.

- Fear works as a motivator. Fear will get players to run hard. Fear will capture their attention for short periods of time. On the other hand, while fear works, it does not work nearly as well as motivating through love and respect.

- Most individuals coach as they were coached. Whatever methods were used with coaches as players is how they at least begin to form their own coaching style.

Regardless of all the people I watched and all the things I tried, the way I was handling conditioning still didn't reflect who I was or wanted to be as a coach. I couldn't reduce my expectations for the level of condition I felt my teams needed to be in to compete at their best. By the same token, I often found myself having to build up some sense of anger or find mistakes and using them as reasons why I was going to run the players hard.

I spent a lot of time trying to find the style that would fit my philosophy and still accomplish the level of conditioning that I felt my teams required to be successful. The "smart" side of me said the goal should be to take things that were important to me and essential for team success (e.g., conditioning) and find a way to make them equally important to the players.

On the other hand, the "positive" side of me said that I had to find a way to take things that are not inherently fun and make them enjoyable. Conditioning and coaching should not be "forced labor" or motivated through fear. In my mind, the choice was clear—I had to shift my thinking. In that regard, I wanted to achieve the following objectives:

- To be in better game condition than any of our opponents.

- To have our condition be a source of pride.

- To not have to be upset to get them to run.

  As such, this is what I believed to be true:

- Being good is a privilege. Having fun for an athlete involves being good.

- The greatest management principle of motivation refers to the fact that things that get rewarded get done, and those things will perpetuate themselves. This precept is especially true if you are rewarding "student-owned behaviors," or choices. Effort is a "student-owned" behavior that is completely within the athlete's control.

- If you reward an OK effort and call it "great," you'll get an OK effort. If you reward a good effort as great, you will get a good effort. On the other hand, if you only reward great effort, you will get great effort, and the great effort will perpetuate itself. Accordingly, if you only reward what you consider "great" or improved effort until it becomes great, then your players will be more likely to reach the desired level. You can always say "that was better," for an improved effort. But do not say "that was great," if it wasn't.

- The best form of reinforcement is positive. The best forms of positive reinforcements are verbal, physical, and love.

My goal, then, became to take what I knew and get what I wanted. Subsequently, I used the following steps to change the way my players looked at conditioning. I introduced the theory by verbally asking them if they believed the following premises (which, in turn, led to the listed conclusion):

⇨ Premise #1. Being in great condition will make you a better player. True or false? Being a better individual player will make us a better team. True or false?

⇨ Premise #2. Conditioning will allow us to have more success. True or false? Conditioning is something the best teams at any level always have. True or false?

⇨ Conclusion: Therefore, conditioning should be looked at as a privilege. True or false?

Once they accepted the aforementioned conclusion, I was able to adapt the following ideas:

- The better practice they had, the more conditioning I would provide for them.

- Effort = praise. Since great work habits are developed from praising effort, the coaches praised all great effort, regardless of time or outcome.

- If you won a competition, you were allowed to run, and if you lost, you did not get to run.

- As coaches, we had to learn to reward our best workers, instead of getting upset at the poor workers. We also had to stop punishing those players who were trying their best, but happened to have been born with an unacceptable level of foot speed, by making them or the whole team run again when they finished last or with a slower-than-established time. The immediate result was that more of these foot-slow players became good workers. If we had some players who continued to give a poor effort, we had made a mistake in squad selection, and they had to be eliminated if they could not (or would not) change their work habits. Giving less than your best effort is a selfish, player-owned decision.

- By positively recognizing and reinforcing great effort, we consistently got great effort. Once you are getting your athletes' best effort, there will be a natural skill progression and an increased level of conditioning.

Motivating Your Athletes Through Positive Conditioning

All factors considered, the actual techniques used to condition your players are not as important as the consistency and reinforcement you employ to motivate your athletes toward their best efforts. Many coaches feel like they must constantly create different conditioning drills to keep their athletes from being bored. On the other hand, we found that we were able to carry over many of the same running sequences that we had used before and just add the new reinforcement techniques. Think of the drills you currently use to condition your team and whether they have provided a sufficient fitness level. See if you can adjust the reinforcement techniques you employ and use the same drills.

No matter what drills we employed for conditioning, the developmental focus of most of these exercises concentrated on cardiovascular fitness (i.e., stamina, aerobic fitness). We then designed the drills around the criteria that we used for building teams, including:

- Depending on each other.
- Achieving tough, common goals.
- Balancing fun and discipline.
- Relying on mutual respect by providing dignity.
- Being positive but demanding in our leadership.
- Encouraging athletes to abide by one single rule – "don't let your teammates down."

Employing Positive Conditioning

Every coach should verbally reinforce great efforts that occur in any of the conditioning activities. One of the most important aspects of positive conditioning is to provide an opportunity for dignity. For example, allow players to take off extra clothing (in football, having the players take their helmets off allows the coaches to see effort on the faces of each player). Yes, they play with their helmets on, but wouldn't you rather see their faces and have them be able to hear your praise? Allow time for players to recover from the previous conditioning effort particularly if it was rigorous or intense (e.g., sprinting), so they can give their best effort. One of the techniques that can be used to ensure that all of your players are able to recover and be ready and willing to give full effort is to have them individually raise their hands when they are prepared for the next conditioning activity. This step allows each player to recover at his own rate. By putting his hand up, it also says, "I commit to full effort."

If you have players who want to excuse themselves from conditioning because they are not feeling well (or for any other reason), let them out. Do not force them to exercise. Conditioning should be a privilege. Do not let them stand there and watch the others engage in the conditioning activities. Rather, have them go in while you give the players who are present full praise for their effort.

"Don't let your teammates down" was the only rule we had for our teams. During conditioning, that rule provides a different incentive for individual players to exercise. Beyond conditioning, that single rule encompasses all areas of athletic behavior and leaves you a wide amount of discretion. It covers such aspects as effort, attention, punctuality, academic progress, and decisions on weekends. "Don't let your teammates down" is a way of reinforcing the fact that the team is relying on each individual to make good choices and that the team is always more important than any individual player.

Selecting the Appropriate Conditioning Drills

The following conditioning drills can be performed to meet the developmental needs of your athletes:

• Timed Running Drill

This drill involves setting a goal to have your players run for a certain amount of time (based upon distance and number of players). During this running, watch for every opportunity to verbally reward effort, but also to identify if any player is not giving an appropriate effort. If you see poor or marginal effort, you should stop the running drill for the entire team. Without publicly singling out who the offender was, the team needs to know that unless every player is committed to an all-out effort, the drill will not continue. Usually, all you have to say is that "at least one player was not giving his best, and the team needs the best effort of EVERY player." "We are depending on you, don't let your teammates down and tomorrow will be another chance to have everyone give their best." All factors considered, the better they want to be as a team, the more it will bother them to be stopped, and the longer they will want to set their time goals. If the point in the conditioning drill where they had to be stopped occurs in the middle of practice, you should just go on to the next section of practice. If it happens at the end of practice, you should declare that practice is done for the day, with the understanding that tomorrows' practice could be better and they would have another opportunity to enhance their level of conditioning at that time.

Similar to cardiovascular exercises, you can employ the same principles to perform strengthening exercises as well. If you tell your players to "do 30 push-ups," there may be some athletes, who no matter how hard they try, can not do 30. On the other hand, there may be some players who are capable of doing many more than 30. For these players, doing 30 push-ups is not even a challenge. But, if you say, "see how many push-ups you can do in 30 seconds," that allows the player who can only do 15 to give his maximum effort and be straining for number 16 at the end of the designated time and be receiving praise for his effort. It also allows the player who is capable of doing 45 push-ups in 30 seconds to demonstrate all the push-ups he is capable of doing, and receive praise for his effort, not his ability to do just 30 push-ups.

- Three-Person Exchange Drill

This drill involves timed running. Most timed running is done using interval training (three- or four-person exchange). In this drill, players line up in groups of three or four, depending on how much rest you want them to have between sprints. If you have an odd number of players and have one line with four individuals, when you want everyone running in groups of three, just combine two players and have them run at the same time (bottom group). In Diagram 5-1, players #1 and #2 remain at one end of the distance (e.g., 30 to 100 yards in sports such as football and soccer or a court-length in sports such as basketball and volleyball), while #3 is positioned on the opposite end of the designated area. In this drill, #1 runs to #3 and stays at that end; #3 runs and tags #2 and stays there; and #2 runs and exchanges with #1. Each player goes through the pattern of run-rest, and run-rest until the designated period of time has expired.

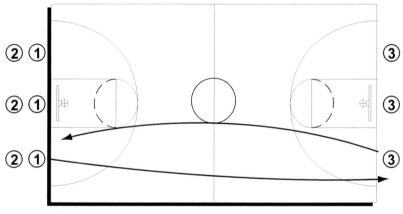

Diagram 5-1

- Half-Court, Back, Full-Court Drill

This drill is the same type of exercise as the previous exercise, only it employs change-of-direction running. In Diagram 5-2, players #1 and #2 line up on the starting line, while player #3 lines up at the opposite end of the area involved. This drill can be done on a basketball court (as shown in Diagram 5-2) or on a field with the distances varied. The first player in each line starts and goes to the half-court line, reverses his direction and sprints back to the place he started, and then reverses his direction again and sprints to the far end to player #3. Player #1 tags #3 and stays there, as #3 goes half-court and back and then full-court to exchange with #2. Players see how many full-effort sprints they can get in during the allotted time.

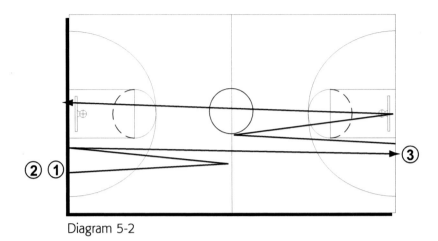

Diagram 5-2

• Individual Maximum Efforts Drill

This drill may be as simple as determining how many sprints each individual player can do during a specific time period. After sprinting, each player should rest so he can go all-out on his next effort. Players will be running the same distances, but at different times, and not on a command. The coach must establish distances and times that are challenging, but possible, and are appropriate to the needs of their sport. Players should challenge themselves to do as many quality-effort sprints as possible in the allotted time. Coaches need to focus on praising the maximum efforts of players who are running, and not get sidetracked by players who are resting. If you are reinforcing correctly, players will normally do everything in their power to hear their name as many times as possible during this time.

If you decide to run this type of conditioning, you should begin this section of your practice by allowing your athletes to set the length of running time for that day. It is wise to discuss with team leaders the value of gradually increasing the time and number of sprints that the team should be required to do with maximum efforts. This style of running allows each player to work to his maximum capacity, depending on how quickly he can recover individually. Vary the recovery times, so that your stronger players get an opportunity for more sprints and your less-conditioned players will still be able to receive praise for the efforts they are able to give. Each player should strive to achieve his personal best and not compare with his teammates. Conducting this drill in this way enables all players to benefit by improving their level of physical condition.

• Run for a Certain Number of Sprints Drill

This drill involves having the team leadership set a goal for the number of untimed sprints they want the team to run on a specific day. Again, you should allow recovery time, praise every great effort, and stop the group if you have anyone who is not putting forth his best effort. It is wise to meet with your team leaders throughout the season and talk about how to set realistic goals, and how and when to increase the number of sprints they are attempting. While this drill is tougher on those players who are not as well-conditioned, adequate recovery time enables them to wait until they are completely ready to run again.

- Run After Being Successful or Winning Drill

This drill involves the unique stipulation that "winners run." One of the biggest psychological changes in this form of reinforcement is the thought of "winners run." Usually, winning prevents players from "having" to run. This drill takes the opposite tact. If you are unsuccessful, you do not get to run. One example of a specific drill where success allows running in basketball is "one-and-one and run." In this drill, if you are interspersing the conditioning throughout practice, and your players are going to shoot free throws for three or four minutes, you would have each player shoot a one-and-one. If a player misses either shot, he gets back in his shooting line. If he makes both attempts of the one-and-one, he gets to run down and back.

- Help Your Buddy Drill

In this drill, individuals get into lines of three or four players at the starting point. On the starting command, the first player in each line (#1) runs the required distance and returns to the starting point. The next player (#2) in line watches his "buddy" who is running. He has the option of stepping in and running for him when he returns to the starting point. You should encourage player #2 to watch the running form, speed, and face on his teammate (#1) who is running. If he is straining, losing form, or struggling to maintain his speed, #2 can raise his hand, offer help ("I've got you buddy"), and decide when to step in. Player #1 must stop and allow #2 to take his place. It is entirely the decision of #2. Player #2 then begins running his sprints. At this point, player #3 has the decision on when to replace #2.

This drill promotes several factors that can help improve conditioning and also build team feeling. The runners should attempt to run as long as possible, without slowing or straining so they will not be replaced. The person waiting should be looking for an opportunity to assist a teammate in trouble. The idea of "helping your buddy" or "not letting your buddy down" is contagious – an attitude that likely will be carried over into other areas of practice and games.

- Ask for Help Drill

This drill is set up exactly the same way as the previous conditioning drill. This time, the first player in each line starts running the set distance on the signal and goes as long as he can without stopping, while giving maximum effort. It is the runner's call for help that allows the next runner to enter the sprint. Unless he asks for help, the next runner must stay and wait his turn. The concept of being able to push yourself and be your own judge on how long you can go is a natural motivator. The idea of trying to increase the number of consecutive sprints you can make before needing help will improve the conditioning level of each individual who pushes himself. The situation of running in a "spotlight" makes it difficult for any player to give less than his best effort.

The concept of being willing to "ask for help" is essential within successful teams. It is OK to say, "I need help, will you step in for me." Frequently, the most difficult aspect of the drill will be to get the runner to surrender. He will try to go too far. This is a dramatic change from an athlete's traditional mentality towards conditioning.

- Weakest Link in the Chain Drill

When the weakest link in the chain drill is employed, it can be done in small groups or large groups. The most effective approach is to have the entire team attempt to reach a specified goal. One example of how this drill could be conducted would be to have all of the team members line up across the starting position. You would then have them interlock elbows or hold hands to create a chain. The running goal is then set, and the team all begins running together on the command. The goal for the team is to reach the running objective without ever breaking the chain (i.e., the weakest link). An example of a possible running goal for football, for example, may be:

- Runners start at the goal line with their hands linked.

- Run to the 10-yard line and stop.

- Turn around, reconnect hands, and, on the command, sprint back to the original start line without breaking the chain.

- Recover, sprint to the 20, turn, and, on command, sprint back.

- Repeat the drill until everyone has run 50 or even 100 yards.

In this scenario, for example, your players will learn early that if they have two slower, heavier runners together, these two "hefty" individuals would often get so far behind that the chain would break. Rather than look toward them as the reason for failure, the stronger, faster players will quickly learn that to prevent the chain from breaking, they must stand on either side of the slower runners and help them along without breaking the link. Again you are not only conditioning your team, while achieving a tough goal, you are also creating a mindset where a more conditioned player wants to help a teammate succeed or assist a teammate who wants to have the whole team accomplish their desired goal.

- Run With Other Teams Drill

If you have another team during your season that is also using the principles of positive conditioning, it can provide additional motivation to combine both programs in the same conditioning drills. Since you are looking for and praising effort, the speed or strength of the participants can be completely different. For example, you can conduct a drill where both genders are combined in sports such as basketball, football, and softball or even where high school athletes are grouped with members of youth teams. In this situation, it is fun for both groups to cheer for each other. Furthermore, they gain an appreciation for the efforts of classmates, regardless of the age, sport, or speed. You can intermix the groups in three- or four-person exchanges. In the process, you can develop a positive attitude and a heightened level of conditioning for your own team, as well as build respect for the efforts of the other team (i.e., program pride and support).

• Winner's Circle Drill

This drill involves a scenario where you set tough, but achievable, goals, so that your team can all end practice in the "winner's circle." Set a goal for each group of runners, so that the stronger runners can help teammates who are not as well-conditioned. Once a particular group has reached its individual goal, the members of the group all go into an area designated as the "winner's circle." The basic objective of the drill is to have the entire team accomplish a set goal and all end up in the circle before time expires. This drill could be conducted in a variety of ways and settings. For example, a group of three basketball players could be required to run a full-speed, half-court, back, full-court sprint and then make both ends of a one-and-one free throw. In football, a group of three or four players could be required to run cross-field sprints, with all players running at the same time. Each group would attempt to run the same set number of sprints in the allotted amount of time. As soon as your group completes the set number, move to the winner's circle and encourage the remaining groups. Occasionally, you can allow those players who finish early to go contribute to a team that has not reached its goal yet. They would then combine their group total to try to reach a set number. Again, you have a group of players working together to achieve a goal, with teammates and coaches encouraging or offering help. Coaches or group leaders should balance the teams to give each group a reasonable opportunity to succeed.

• Eliminator Drill

In traditional conditioning practices, the first several players who finish are done and are allowed to go into the locker room, while all of the other players are forced to go back and run another sprint. This procedure usually continues until only the slowest runners are left.

The other method that is often used to conduct this drill involves a scenario where if the whole team doesn't finish under a certain time, then the whole team runs again. This method does nothing to promote team unity, and usually results in faster players being upset at their teammates, who just happen to not be gifted with speed and therefore cause the group to have to run again (i.e., forced labor, based upon outcome, not effort). The faster players can coast and still make the required time. On the other hand, the slower players may be giving everything they have and still have no chance to finish under the time limit, regardless of how much they try.

The eliminator drill can be conducted in a manner similar to the "winner's run" drill, where the players who finish last in a race are "eliminated" from further running, while the fastest runners can continue to condition.

One of the most powerful drills at your disposal is the eliminator. Coaches can choose any sprint distance they want (e.g., 40-yard sprint, crosscourt 16's, half-court, full-court), as long as the distance is equal for all competitors. You should use this drill sparingly (i.e., two or three times per season). You should only use this drill if the whole team has bought in to your conditioning program. On the day that this drill is performed, you should have already done other conditioning exercises. For the first time in the conditioning process, players are eliminated, based upon their speed.

In football, for example, all of the players would begin on the goal line, with the finish line 40 yards away. On the start signal, all players sprint for the finish line. Coaches praise all of the maximum efforts, but watch to see who the last five players across the line are. Those five are eliminated but do not leave the field. Instead, they join the coaches as encouragers for the players remaining in the drill. The players left in the drill then jog back to the goal line and recover at their own rate. Each athlete commits to maximum effort when he has recovered by raising his hand. Once all hands are raised, the coach gives the signal to start the next sprint. Again, the last five finishers are eliminated and join the group of encouragers. The remaining players repeat the process of jogging back and recovering. Coaches eliminate players – five at a time – until the group reaches a total of 10 players. At that point, the coaches reduce the participants two at a time, until they reach the final four. When the group is reduced to only four players, the coaches then eliminate one player at a time. The other players are employed to form a tunnel for the final players to sprint through. At the conclusion of each sprint, the remaining players in the drill are allowed as much time as necessary to recover before being required to sprint again. The players who have been eliminated are commended by everyone if they have given their best effort. By the time you get to the final two, the fastest players have run quite a few competitive sprints. After the final two have run against each other, you can then give the winner the option of running one by himself after he has recovered. Most players in this situation usually choose to run one sprint alone.

Players often dive for the line to try to keep from being one of the last five or to get to the next round. We once had the two final players both simultaneously dive for the line to have the privilege of running one sprint by themselves. Occasionally, the final player, running by himself, will dive across the finish line as the tunnel of teammates cheers him through the 40 yards.

- Push Day Drill

A "push day" can be scheduled once you completely believe that your team has bought in to the positive-conditioning concept and is doing everything in their power to push themselves and help each other. In other words, they have become a great team. For teams that reach this level, coaches can decide to schedule a "push day" (usually, only on a once-a-year basis). In this drill, you go through a normal practice, followed by the most strenuous conditioning session of the year. At the conclusion of the conditioning, you bring your players together and talk about how much of conditioning is mental and how they are capable of so much more than they think or have ever done. When they think they have just completed the most difficult conditioning of their life, you then ask them if they believe they are capable of more. Then you start over and repeat the entire conditioning section, doubling the most strenuous day of the year. When I was coaching, it was a tradition for our teams to anticipate and look forward to being challenged, knowing that the coaches must really think they are a special team to qualify for a "push day." Most teams will look back on that day as a standard for not quitting, for achieving a goal that they did not believe was possible, and as a unifying moment. It is something they are proud to have accomplished. It becomes part of who they are as a team and as an individual athlete. It is something that they will remember long after all the games are finished. In my personal experience, athletes from 20 years ago still say, "coach, I will never forget push day—that was physically the hardest day of my life, but it is a great memory."

Making Positive Conditioning Work for Your Team

Utilize your imagination and creativity to develop drills that serve your conditioning purposes, and then employ the motivation principles of rewarding effort. You can use almost any conditioning drill, just change the focus of the verbal reinforcement from outcome to effort.

The results will speak for themselves. Your most talented athletes will have a chance to be both your best workers and the best conditioned. This situation is what you need if you are going to rely on them to carry the physical load for the team. Possibly even more importantly, because they get their efforts praised, this approach to conditioning will enable your weaker athletes to be in better condition and to be able to feel good about themselves and their contribution to the team. Your bigger or slower players will love the concept of rewarding effort and will enjoy being part of this system of reinforcement. As such, they will hate to be cut out of the "eliminator," and want to continue running.

One of the key elements in the success of the positive conditioning concept is that once your team has completely bought in to this philosophy, you should give them ownership. Rather than viewing the situation as, "look what I have done as a coach," the player-oriented focus is on, "look at who you have become." The players are the ones doing the work, while trying not to let their teammates down. They are the ones who look at conditioning as a privilege and see the benefits of being part of an unselfish unit.

You will find with teams that have made a conscious choice to buy in to this concept that the worst punishment you can give them is to not allow them to run. As such, if you have a practice where there is poor effort or poor concentration, you simply do not allow the team to condition. Just like positive effort and behavior, poor effort or concentration are "student-owned" choices.

This conditioning concept also requires a complete buy-in from your entire coaching staff, not just you, as the head coach. Once you have gone in this direction, you can not revert back to previous methods and philosophies of conditioning your team. One instance of getting upset during practice and saying to your team, "that was bad, get on the line, and you are going to run" will cause you and your system to lose credibility.

If you are able to make the transition from a traditional approach to conditioning to a positive-conditioning philosophy, the following will be true:

- You will not believe how hard your players will work.

- You will not believe how they support and encourage each other.

- You will not believe how much closer they become when they are pulling for each other instead of having to run as punishment for mistakes or outcome.

- You will not believe how much harder you are able to push your team.

- You will not believe how much better they feel about themselves and their team as they leave the practice area.

- You will not believe how much different you feel as an encourager, rather than a slave driver.

In a profession that has lasting value to life, recall the previous discussion concerning the point that most individuals coach as they were coached. In turn, if you are able to make this one change, consider what you are doing for the next generation of coaches, as well as for helping to create positive memories for your current athletes.

Tradition #24—Line of Commitment

❑ *Lessons from this tradition*: Do not step on the practice field until you are ready and committed.

As your players leave the locker room and approach the field or court, have a line on the ground that they have to cross right before they arrive at the practice site. Each player needs to pause at the line and think before he enters the practice area and recommit to the Core Covenants of the team. Players who cross the line have said with the first step onto the practice area that they are committed to give their best to subscribe to the beliefs of the team. With teams who are in the beginning stages of development, it is a good idea to make a list of your Core Covenants on a sign that is placed right before players cross the line to enter the field or court. Another method that accomplishes the same thing in a powerful way is to have a coach at the line to hear each player say "I commit to full effort and attention," or "I commit to not letting my teammates down" or to whatever your Core Covenants are. The line of commitment tradition also enhances the ability of coaches to get focused on practice and away from anything else that has gone on during the day.

Tradition #25—Tryouts *
(*Submitted by Greg Oldham, head girl's basketball coach;
Coupeville High School, Coupeville, WA)

❑ *Lessons from this tradition*: Welcome to our team. Establishing senior leadership and modeling work habits.

Our first three days of practice are called "tryouts," even though we don't often cut anyone (and if we do, it has everything to do with attitude or behavior rather than skill). During the teaching portions of the tryouts, players are grouped across grade levels so that they begin to form connections across classes. The seniors are utilized as leaders and demonstrators to help set them up as the acknowledged leaders of our program. Tryouts consist of physical tests and a scrimmage portion, and we try to "stack the deck" in favor of the seniors—we group our scrimmage teams by class, hoping that the seniors beat the freshmen and sophomores handily. The seniors are also familiar with the tests (and have probably been preparing for them), so they tend to score better than the freshmen and sophomores.

Tradition #26—New Years Eve Practice

❑ *Lessons from this tradition*: You can successfully focus and practice at any time. You are in a place where my family, coach and teammates know you are safe. There are good ways to celebrate and have fun.

Schedule a practice from 10 PM until midnight on New Years Eve. Immediately after practice, have a party in the gym or on campus for your players and guests so that the player's parents know where their kids are that night. Provide a positive activity on a night when kids are looking for things to do. Allow them to invite friends to the after practice party. This tradition provides positive alternatives for New Years Eve. It can be done with just your team, or with both the boys and the girls teams, with all the teams in season, or for all the athletes in your school. Parents, seniors, and coaches should be involved in the planning of activities and in supervising the activities.

Tradition #27—Pre-Practice Two-Minute Warning Horn

❏ *Lessons from this tradition*: Be on time—no excuses; you had a two-minute warning. The team starts on time.

If you want your practices to begin exactly on time, this tradition can help you. Assign a manager or coach to blow a horn or whistle to let everyone know that practice will begin in two minutes with all the players who are on time and without any player who is late.

Tradition #28—Hard Hat of the Week Award

❏ *Lessons from this tradition*: Identification and reward for effort in practice.

Get a hard hat or two, place school decals or something that identifies your program on the side, and award the hard hats to the hardest workers in practice that week. The player(s) wear them to and from practice and possibly at school. Coaches and/or captains can make the decision on who should receive the "Hard Hat of the Week."

Tradition #29—Sunrise Service

❏ *Lessons from this tradition*: You can focus and practice hard and effectively at any time day or night.

Once a year, schedule an early morning practice that begins at 4 AM. This practice is designed to teach individuals that they can play at any time or under any conditions. It can be done by having players arrive on their own or by having them spend the night together with coaches on the field, in the gym, or at a central location in town. The night before can be used to do a service project for the school or community so that the focus of the effort is not on a sleep-over as much as serving someone else, getting up early, and focusing on practice. This tradition is a great opportunity for team cohesiveness and bonding. Supervision has to be sufficient, boundaries must be established, and approval obtained. When the practice ends at 6 AM, have breakfast ready for the athletes as soon as they have showered and changed for school. This situation may be a good time to have parents or even the principal help coaches prepare the breakfast. During the school day following the practice, no exceptions should be allowed for missed school, inattentiveness, or lack of effort in any class. The fastest way to kill this tradition is to have teachers complain that the athletes were not good students following the early practice. The players owe it to the teams that will follow them to be at their best on this day.

Tradition #30—Name the Drill After Me

❏ *Lessons from this tradition*: Having fun is being good (i.e., skilled with full effort). Effort is praised and rewarded on this team. Names from the history of the program are remembered.

Instead of calling drills by their traditional names, such as "deny the flash post drill", "cat and mouse drill," etc., name the drills after the best player to have played for the school to ever perform the drill. Drills are just as easily recognized as long as they are given a specific name. For example, a particular drill could become the "Dino Simone drill" and stay by that name until someone comes along and can perform the drill at a higher level of expertise. Having a drill named after you is an honor, and says that you are the best person to ever perform that drill in the history of the program. It tells your players that performing the drills is important to you and to the history of the program. It tells them that this drill has been successfully employed for an extended period of time. It becomes a source of pride to have a drill named for you. All factors considered, players will learn better and faster if they are trying to get a drill named after them or thinking about the person for which the drill was named. Players will ask, "Who is that guy?" Such an inquiry will give you a chance to acquaint them with some person from your coaching career. Players will come back after a few years, and one of the first things they will ask is, "Is that drill still named after me?" Every time you introduce a drill that you are going to use for the first time, you can call it by the technical name (e.g., two-strike drill). In this situation, every player will realize that this drill hasn't been given an official name, and that by the end of season, it will be named after somebody on this team.

Tradition #31—Touch the Past

❑ *Lessons from this tradition*: To start your engine before practice. To link you to the past where something great happened. To focus on what is important about this team or this experience.

Place a sign or plaque on the edge of your field or court that the players have to walk by at the beginning and end of practice. The tradition is that every player touches the monument whenever he passes it. The item to be touched may be as simple as a shamrock above the door or a sign that every player has to slap when leaving the locker room (e.g., something that proclaims a motivational message like "play like a champion today") or as meaningful as the plaque located at the entrance to the practice field at West Point that reads, "I want an officer for a secret and dangerous mission. I want a West Point football player" (General George C. Marshall). The key point is that players are touching the exact spot where the teammates from past years have placed their hands.

Tradition #32—The Supreme Court

❑ *Lessons from this tradition*: Making fun of each other can be done in a way that is enjoyable for everyone. Everyone has to pay the piper. A light-hearted method of keeping teammates in line.

At the beginning of the season, "judges" are elected or appointed by the coaches and team. On a relatively large team, the number of judges could total at least three. These judges become The Supreme Court for the team. The judges "hold court," and can fine up to 25 cents for any infraction they deem important to the team. It needs to kept light, so having judges with a sense of humor who can be accepted by everyone is essential. Examples of fineable offenses may include the following: a player not smiling or not tipping his hat when the player passed the judge, too many girl (boy) friends, a player not eating his vegetables at lunch, a player seen on the weekend not helping his mom with the groceries, offensive smelling socks, etc. Coaches are also fair game. Coaches and captains need to be aware of not carrying this too far.

Tradition #33—Combative Day*
(*Submitted by Mark Perry, head football coach;
Snohomish High School, Snohomish, WA)

❏ *Lessons from this tradition*: Fun. Competing away from the normal drills. Team spirit.

On the last practice during preseason two-a-days or to break up the routine of practice, coaches can schedule a combative day. The team is divided up into two or more teams to compete against each other in a variety of short, safe, combative games. Winners advance in a tournament format until a champion is declared. Team points may be kept for the top four places. Examples of the type of combative games that can be conducted include:

• "Towel pull"–two players grasp the same towel and attempt to pull each other out of a circle.

• "Neck pull"–two players start on their knees, facing each other, with their eyes up. They have a harness hooked to their heads that is strung tightly between them. The goal is to use your neck muscles to pull on your opponent. The first player to drop their head and have the harness come off loses.

• "Aardvark"–four or five players from each team get into a circle (e.g., a wrestling mat or a circle drawn on the ground). They must stay on their knees and cannot do anything to endanger another player. Coaches should be particularly sensitive to stop any activity that is potentially dangerous to the player' knees, shoulders, and elbows. One team is designated the "aards", while the other is the "varks." The only thing the players can say while they're in the game is the name of the their team, either "aard" or "vark." The goal is for one team to throw, pull, or drive everyone from the other team completely out of the circle. Coaches must be constantly judging, because if a player has one toe or one finger still in the circle, they are OK. The pile gets messed up quickly and the only way you can call for help or tell someone that you are on their team, is to call out which team you are on ("aard, aard, aard" or "vark, vark"). The sound alone is hilarious. If anyone says anything other than "aard" or "vark," they are out.

- "Rooster fight"—each player is matched against an opponent of equal weight and strength. The two players representing opposing teams enter the circle standing on one foot and holding one of their ankles with their hand. The goal is to knock the other person off balance to the point where that individual falls down, goes out of the circle, or lets go of their ankle. Any of those three occurrences ends the match. Every player on each team has one match, and the team with the most total matches, wins.

Tradition #34—Link Up

- *Lessons from this tradition*: The team is only as strong as its weakest link. Work together. Pull for each other. Appreciate teammates' efforts to keep up together. Rely on each other.

Set up at least one conditioning drill that the team can do while holding onto a rope. The players run the designated distance or for the specified time while linked together. Some players may need to be pulled along, while others may have to slow slightly and pull a teammate. The goal is to complete the running without breaking the chain. To avoid injury, coaches need to set the drill up so no one will be falling or tripping over a teammate or getting rope burns.

6

Last Practice Traditions

The last practice of the season or of a career should have special significance. Coaches who value practice need to establish traditions that honor the last practice.

Tradition #35—My Best Memory

❑ *Lessons from this tradition*: Acknowledging teammates. Remembering the good things before the season is completely over. Getting the underclassmen to begin to think about the memories they will have. Recognizing the good things to come. Closure.

About a week before the end of the season, talk to the seniors and tell them that they will have an opportunity to talk about their best memories of being on the team or in the program for the three years. This time should provide them a chance to be thoughtful, concise and prepared. Set up a time at the beginning or the end of practice to allow the seniors to speak to the rest of the team (bring in everyone from all levels of the program) about the special memories that they have.

Tradition #36—The Most Influential Person In My Life

❑ *Lessons from this tradition*: Being thankful for the people who have helped you along the way. Reconnect with the past.

At the last practice or during the whole last week of practice, allow each of the seniors to talk about the most influential person in their life. You may not want to place any restrictions on who this person is, or you may want to have it be someone outside of their family, such as their most influential teacher, etc. You may want to have each senior give his thoughts just in front of the team, or you may want to have the senior bring the person who has influenced him to the practice to hear what is being shared with the team.

Tradition #37—Final Sprints

❑ *Lessons from this tradition*: Closure. One final time to be in front of the team. The emotion of doing something for the last time. Special meaning.

Form a tunnel with your whole team and have the seniors run one at a time through the tunnel on their last sprint. One last chance to demonstrate effort and love. After they have run individually, have the seniors run one final sprint as a group holding hands. When they are finished, have the team surround them for one last "endorsement."

Tradition #38—Final Lap*
(* Submitted by Bill Kramer, head football coach; Naples High School, Naples, FL)

❑ *Lessons from this tradition*: Saying goodbye. Emotion involved in closure to a great memory.

Each of the seniors runs one victory lap around the field. The rest of the team circles the field. The seniors run by the freshmen first, then by the sophomores and then by the juniors and finally by the coaches. After completing their lap, the seniors gather together and move to the rest of the team with the coaches.

Tradition #39—Piggy Back*
(* Submitted by Bill Kramer, head football coach; Naples High School, Naples FL)

❑ *Lessons from this tradition*: Identifying an underclassman with whom you have a special connection. You can count the underclassman to carry you when you need it. Tribute to the work you have done to make this a great team and this a special season.

The seniors can pick any underclassman and have them carry them the last twenty yards off the field. It is done respectfully and honorably to demonstrate thanks to the senior. Another option is to use three or four underclassmen and have them carry the senior off on their shoulders.

Tradition #40—A Piece of My Life–A Piece of My Experience

❑ *Lessons from this tradition*: Taking a physical piece of your athletic experience with you for the rest of your life.

Have a ceremony at the end of the last practice to let the seniors take part of the season with them. Coaches set the standard for what can be used for each senior to take with them. It may be a piece of turf, a portion of the net, or any memento associated with the sport. Coaches need to be creative and set boundaries about what the seniors can take or the seniors might abuse their options.

Tradition #41—Senior Memory Video

❑ *Lessons from this tradition*: Saying goodbye. Linking up with the past experiences of seniors in the program. Enjoy the journey.

Make, edit, and play videotape of all the seniors talking about the experiences they had while playing the sport at your school. Edit in at least one positive play from a game or of the senior being introduced at the final game. Coaches may want to play videotapes from years past before the final week of practice. Tapes of championship teams from the past can be shown at the beginning of the season to get seniors and the whole team thinking about enjoying the journey on which they are about to embark. Every senior who participates in the presentations should receive their own copy of the video or the CD-ROM.

7

Pre-Game Traditions

Tradition #42–Kids on the Field (Court) for the National Anthem

❑ *Lessons from this tradition*: The National Anthem is something special. The kids can identify with a player of their choice. The players interact with fans. Little kids setting their goals to become a future player or even a player on that team when they grow up.

After the players are introduced and have taken the field (or court) and before the National Anthem is played, have the children in attendance gather at one location. Then, on a signal or announcement, have the children come out on the field and stand next to a player or group of players, coaches or officials of their choice. If you want to include your whole team, your players can go to go to designated spots on the field or court and stand in small groups so that everyone is going to have some children next to them, and no one is left out. At the conclusion of the Anthem, the players slap hands with each of the children in their group before they return to their seats.

Tradition #43–Tunnel of Former Players

❑ *Lessons from this tradition*: The past is important. You are still part of this program. Thanks for carrying on the traditions of the past.

Either for one special game or for every game of the season, have the former players line up to welcome players onto the field or court. Any former player in attendance should also feel free to come into the locker room at any time. Former players who want to bring their own children with them to greet the current team are sending the message that "some day, if you are as fortunate as I was, you will play in this program."

Tradition#44—Fan Behavioral Expectation Card

❑ *Lessons from this tradition*: In our program, our fans are expected to behave correctly.

If you want to improve fan behavior at your games, a message from your players will carry great power. Hand out a card with the purchase of a ticket that says something like, "The athletes in this league (or school) have made a commitment to character and the spirit of the game. Please help them by modeling appropriate behavior." I have seen a school with problem adults in their crowd help control the actions of these misguided individuals by having student leaders give out cards extolling good behavior. These schools also have their designated athletes award a yellow card and red card, like soccer, to misbehaving adults. The yellow card asks these adults to "please model appropriate behavior", while the red card says, "your behavior is not acceptable, please leave." A red or a yellow card doesn't have to be used very often before people get the message that their behavior is out of line.

Tradition #45—Back-Door Gang

❑ *Lessons from this tradition*: For the kids, a positive connection with this team (e.g., "I can't wait to be part of this experience"). A continuing a relationship with the players they met at summer camp. For the varsity players, small eyes are watching you.

Prior to the game, any kid who attended the school's summer camp and has their camp shirt on is welcome to get into the back door of the locker room for the pre-game meeting. A manager or coach opens the back door for a brief period of time (e.g., five minutes–6:55 - 7:00) prior to the pre-game meeting and then closes the door at a designated time. The parents can walk their child to the door to make sure they are safe and can get in to the locker room. Every kid who is present at the designated time can get into the game without paying and listen to the pre-game meeting with the team as long as they are respectful and quiet.

Tradition #46—Human Welcome Tunnel*
(* Submitted by Jeff Bryson, head coach; Darrington High School, Darrington WA)

❑ *Lessons from this tradition*: The community supports the team. Athletes can't wait to be part of this experience. For the players, how much support they have in their community.

All young people in attendance are allowed onto the field or court to form a tunnel for players to run through prior to the game. Darrington High School has an old "Hoosiers style" gymnasium with a raised grandstand. As the players enter the court, they circle the floor and slap hands with everyone from the community who is within reach.

Tradition #47—Pep Band Leads a Parade to the Game

❑ *Lessons from this tradition*: Community spirit. Everyone is in this together. Everyone is part of the same team.

The pep band starts to play at a place in town several blocks from the school and at a designated time. Initially, they play the school fight song. After one song in place, they begin to march toward the field or gym. The sound of the band playing signals the community that the games are just about to begin. Once at the school, the band leads the team onto the playing field. If you want to extend the tradition more to your community, anyone who has an instrument and can play the school fight song is welcome to join the pep band.

Tradition #48—Special Captains

❑ *Lessons from this tradition*: Inclusion.

Coaches or captains can select any special needs children from the community to serve as honorary captains. Individuals who are selected wear a jersey and go out with the captains to meet the officials before the game.

Tradition #49—Everything Positive Video–"Nothing But Net" On Game Day *
(* Submitted by Pat Fitterer, head boys' basketball coach;
Sehome High School, Bellingham, WA)

❑ *Lessons from this tradition*: Seeing yourself succeeding. Having a positive mental image.

Edit game tape to produce a short individual tape of each player's performance and one of the team. The individual player tape is just him making positive plays (e.g., five minutes of every shot going in, even if it is the same shot). The team tape is segments of the team from a game or practice, during a time when they were executing everything well. Videos are watched to start each practice or right before the game so those players can visualize experiencing success.

Tradition #50—Special Delivery

❑ *Lessons from this tradition*: You are special to your coaches. Get ready to play your best game. The team needs your best.

Coaches write notes to each player that can be used at different times during the season. The note should contain something special for each player (e.g., how the players have helped the team, a time when they made a difference, a quote that reminds you of them, etc.). Personal notes are effective at any time but particularly during pre-game, before big games, over the summer (when you want to keep the players focused) or before the players' last game. It is more effective if the notes are unexpected. They can be delivered to the players in class, placed in their locker, mailed or even hand delivered to their home, etc.

Tradition #51—Home Visit

❑ *Lessons from this tradition*: The coach cares about you. Get ready to be at your best.

Before a game when the team is really going to need a particular player to be at his best, do a home visit. Call the home and ask when it would be a good time for you to come over for a few minutes. The message can be simple and short. You are proud of him for the following reasons….You trust him and his teammates trust him…. Everyone is counting on him. Try to do at least one home visit for each player or at least every senior on your team regardless of how talented that player is.

8

Post-Game Traditions

Tradition #52—Run the Bases–Score the Goal

❏ *Lessons from this tradition*: Attachment to the team. Community involvement.

When the game ends, allow anyone who wants to participate to come down to the field or court and run the bases, shoot a three-pointer, take a shot on goal, catch a pass, etc.

Tradition #53—Parent/Child Clinic

❏ *Lessons from this tradition*: Attachment to the team by the community. Provide a chance for the parent and child to connect with the help of your team.

At the conclusion of your game, provide a hands-on 10-minute skills clinic for the community. Parents and their children can come down to the field and get skill instruction from members of the coaching staff and team. Each week can focus on a different skill and/or a character lesson. This tradition can also be undertaken several times during the year after a practice. One of the objectives of the tradition is to teach the parent how to teach a skill, what to watch for when they are correcting their child's efforts to learn the skill and how to support the child in transferring the character lesson into their daily life. Daily character lessons are available at the website, www.NAIA.org —Champions of Character.

Tradition #54—Award Positive Fan Behavior

❏ *Lessons from this tradition*: Positive behavior when you are fan can be seen and rewarded. This behavior is what we stand for as a team and a school both, on the floor and in the stands.

In order to promote good game behavior by fans (both home and visitors), at the conclusion of the game (or during the last timeout), identify fans (one or two, or a family) who have displayed outstanding support and encouragement of their team without demeaning opponents or criticizing officials. The announcer can introduce them to the crowd as "sportsman of the game." Work with a local pizza dealer to have pizza delivered during the contest and to game management, who then awards the pizza to the fans who are chosen. T-shirts can also be used as a reward for exceptional fan behavior.

Tradition #55—Spotlighting *

❑ *Lessons from this tradition*: Public acknowledgement of a job well done. The power of positive praise. Identifying positive character traits.

Spotlighting is a form of public praise. Time can be set aside to spotlight before practice, during practice, after practice, and before games. The most effective time to spotlight, however, is after games. Spotlighting is done by having one teammate or a coach make a positive statement about a member of the team in front of the group. When your athletes become comfortable speaking about one another in public, it can be a good idea to allow parents, former team members, friends, extended family, or staff to come to the post-game, spotlighting session. Spotlighting must be specific to the theme that is being featured that week. Only athletes and coaches are allowed to speak. Furthermore, not everyone has to be recognized to be effective.

An example of post-game spotlighting would be to have a coach identify a player for something he has done that week that models the selected character theme for that period of time. For example, "I would like to spotlight Jim for the *unselfishness* he showed in practice by being willing to accept the role of a new position." In turn, Jim then "spotlights" a teammate for an example of unselfishness. Each player needs to have thought ahead of time about who and what he would spotlight in case he is called upon. The coach can allow the comments to go as long as they are meaningful, sincere, and on target. The coach terminates the spotlighting at a time of his choosing. During this period of public praise, individual behavioral changes can be recognized and relationships (e.g., coach/player, player/player) are enhanced.

During a recent season, head girl's basketball coach Greg Oldham (Coupeville High School; Coupeville, WA) invited parents into the locker room to observe the spotlighting ritual. After the parents were a bit more comfortable, we "flipped the script" on them and had players spotlight their parents one night and had players spotlight someone else's parents another night.

Tradition #56—Spread the Attention

❑ *Lessons from this tradition*: The spotlight needs to be shared. Acknowledge the role of teammates in making the team successful. Respond to the media in a way that always reflects the Core Covenants of the team.

---

* More complete information on this topic can be found in the book, *Teaching Character Through Sport*, by Bruce Brown; Monterey, CA: Coaches Choice; 2003; pp 72-73.

Make a rule that when one player is interviewed after the game (usually the "star" of the game) that he always needs to have the name of at least one other teammate in the article written about him.

Tradition #57—How Many Points Did You Get?

❑ *Lessons from this tradition*: The focus is always on the team.

One of the first things most players are asked at the conclusion of the game is, "How many did you get?" Ask each of your players to respond by interpreting the word "you" to mean the plural for team. So, instead of answering with the total number of points that individual scored personally, each player responds with the number of points the team scored. In a game that ends 84-71, the player who personally scored 2 points or 22 points answers the question of "How many did you score?" by saying "84".

Tradition #58—Cake and Cookies for Our Opponents*
(* Submitted by Greg Oldham, head girl's basketball coach; Coupeville High School, Coupeville, WA)

❑ *Lessons from this tradition*: You are our respected guests when you play at our school.

If you were to talk to our opponents and the officials, they probably would refer to us as the "cake-and-cookie" school. When I arrived in this new league, we started the tradition of the "victory cake." I got this tradition from my high school football coach, Sid Otton of Tumwater. For every game, one player brings a cake. If our opponent beats us, our captains take the cake into their locker room to congratulate them and thank them for making us better. When we win, we eat the cake. We include our parents and the young kids we work with on Saturdays in this celebration.

For every home game, a player makes cookies– a couple of small plates for the officials and a couple of dozen cookies for our opponents. We believe that both our opponents and the officials are our honored guests when they come to our gym. As such, we want to show them how much we appreciate their efforts in making us better. I've seen a great change in our sportsmanship in the three years I've been at Coupeville High School. It is hard to be unsportsmanlike to someone for whom you've baked and given cookies. Other teams in our league (at least three of the five last season) have also incorporated this tradition. Players from another high school recently brought us a cake and a big card at tri-districts last season, even though we weren't playing them.

9

Last-Game Traditions

Tradition #59—Senior Night

❏ *Lessons from this tradition*: You have been important to this program, and your efforts are appreciated.

Before the last home game of the season, provide some time to honor the seniors in your program. Players are introduced and come to the middle of the field or court with their parents. Flowers, action pictures, highlight videos, or other gifts are given to the family from the coaches.

This time is also a period where the honored player can have other people who have been instrumental in his career be part of the celebration. For example, former coaches, teachers, or individuals about whom they have strong feelings can all be part of the group introduced. It is a good idea to include one current teacher whom each player most respects to be involved in the ceremony. In some settings, seniors can be introduced and can enter by walking through the crowd, giving them a chance to thank the people who have been supporting them from the stands all year.

Tradition #60—Action Pictures

❏ *Lessons from this tradition*: Each player is important to you, to the team and to the school.

During the season, hire a professional photographer to come to a game and shoot action pictures of each of your players, making sure that you get plenty of pictures of the seniors. A good photographer can often take pictures that normal cameramen could never get. These photos become treasures for the senior's whole family. Framed pictures can be presented at the last game.

Tradition #61—Thank You Letters

❏ *Lessons from this tradition*: Demonstrating thankfulness to people in your life.

Have your seniors write a letter of thanks to the people whom they appreciate and who have been influential and instrumental in their lives. Letters can be written to parents, teachers, teammates, etc. When the seniors are introduced at the final game, they can present the letters (and/or a flower) to those people who have helped them along the way.

10

Traditions that Involve the Community

Tradition #62—Adopt a Grandparent

❏ *Lessons from this tradition*: Respect for elders. Community involvement.

Each player or each team can "adopt" a person from a local retirement home. These "adoptees" become part of the team, help with practice, sit on the bench during games, and assist wherever they can. Every community typically has a number of older people who have the energy and expertise to contribute in some meaningful way to a team and who can help bring perspective (i.e., insight) to a team. In turn, the "senior citizens" may find it invigorating to be around some young people and a team going through a season.

Tradition #63—Book Mark Club

❏ *Lessons from this tradition*: Relate to the younger members of the community in a way that places importance on being a student and an athlete. Motivate and reward younger students who are making the effort to improve academically.

Find a method to reward effort or academics in the feeder schools. Set up a program with the local elementary schools and/or classrooms where if a student reads a certain number of books or is making an extra effort to improve their academics, they are given "bookmarks" with the high school or college logo. The teacher can simply recognize students for this award who are making special effort. This program gives the teacher more motivational credibility and may also tie the teacher with the team. The bookmark could also serve as a ticket to a game or as a season pass as long as the student attends the game with a paying adult.

Tradition #64—Buck a Dunk for Charity

❑ *Lessons from this tradition*: Give back to the community.

Every dunk (or other designated occurrence during a game, such as three-point shot, shut out, ace, interception, touchdown pass, etc.) that one of your players makes during the season is a chance to give money back to your community. Have your team go out into the community and ask entities (businesses and individuals) to pledge a dollar or more for every dunk recorded by the home team. As the pledges are received, add up the entire total per dunk and have the total posted on a portable scoreboard. Then, assign a student to flip over to the new amount of money raised every time a dunk occurs. Money can go to a worthwhile cause (e.g., food bank, toys for tots, etc.).

Tradition #65—Christmas Joy

❑ *Lessons from this tradition*: Give back to the community. Become a giving person. Realize that there are many people in your community who need and will appreciate the smallest gifts.

Have your team engage in a charitable act, such as buy, bring and help decorate a Christmas tree for an assisted living home or a family in need. Another possibility would be to raise money to buy as many trees as possible for the same group of people. The team could also adopt a family that has children to make sure that the children receive Christmas gifts that they may never have had without the efforts of the team.

Tradition #66—Change for Life

❑ *Lessons from this tradition*: We can use our games to help people in need. Give back to the community.

Place a container at the gate or the concession stand at your home games where people can place their extra change into the bucket. The money will be used to help others (e.g., a family in need, Christmas presents for needy children, etc.).

Tradition #67—Saturday Morning Basketball*
(*Submitted by Greg Oldham, head girl's basketball coach;
Coupeville High School, Coupeville, WA)

❑ *Lessons from this tradition*: Give back to the community. See the game through the eyes of others.

When I first came to Coupeville, the team was not used to practicing on Saturdays (our games are played on Tuesday and Fridays). I knew if we were to improve, we needed to get in the gym one more day a week. Because I didn't want the possibility of being confronted by an open rebellion, I found a way to get my players working on basketball, doing things that our community has grown to embrace. For example, on Saturday mornings we work with elementary students on their fundamental basketball skills for about two hours. Directly after this, we play wheelchair basketball with our local wheelchair basketball team. Although both of these activities are optional for my players, they enjoy doing them so much that we get nearly everyone out helping and improving their own skills (especially when they play in a wheelchair). In addition, it has been a public relations dream for us with our community.

Tradition #68—Born to Be an Athlete

❑ *Lessons from this tradition*: Connect and celebrate with the community.

Every time a boy or girl is born in your town, an item associated with the athletic program, such as a basketball, football, volleyball, knit hat with the high school logo on it, etc., is given to the child. A player can visit the hospital and deliver the ball to the child's parents. In addition, a coach can bring "eligibility papers" or a certificate for the future athlete.

Tradition #69—The Best Seat in the House

❑ *Lessons from this tradition*: Thanks for being such a great supporter of the high school. Your efforts are appreciated.

Place a recliner or an easy chair at the end of your bench for a special supporter or community leader. Announce the name of the fan chosen for the honor or if you have a specific person that has been a great fan for a long time, you can award them a "lifetime seat." The chair can be assigned on either a rotating or permanent basis.

Tradition #70—Host Coaches or Community Captains

❑ *Lessons from this tradition*: Helping support the school and the teams.

Get volunteers from your community to act as host coaches for the season. The host coaches provide for the needs of the home or visiting team before, during, or after the game. They sit on the home bench during the game. A list of potential duties or expectations should be developed to make the jobs easier. Along the same line of promotion, people from the community can be nominated by the team to be an honorary captain for the week. The honorary captains position can be filled by anyone from the community (e.g., grandparents, teachers, children, business people, supporters, etc.).

Tradition #71—Saturday Morning Football League*
(*Submitted by Mark Perry, head football coach;
Snohomish High School, Snohomish WA)

❑ *Lessons from this tradition*: Personal connection with the kids of the community. Perspective for the players and coaches. Get back to reality after either a win or a loss.

Win or lose, the varsity players and coaches from the football team conduct a Saturday morning 6-on-6 flag football league for the kids of the community. The coaches referee, and the players wear their game jerseys (the opposite color from the one they wore in the game the night before) and coach the teams. The youth teams wear a T-shirt jersey with the number of their favorite player. The teams play a round-robin format. Every Saturday begins with 20 minutes of stretching and instruction before the games so that the skills and terminology are being taught. If the youth-league players wear a Saturday morning team jersey to home games, they get in free.

Tradition #72—Little Brother, Little Sister

❑ *Lessons from this tradition*: Give back to the community. Help change a life. Get the perspective of the teacher. Modeling.

Have each class of players adopt a little brother or sister from a local elementary school. Elementary school teachers can supply a list of kids who need direction or academic assistance. Players can become reading partners, study buddies, or lunch pals and work one-on-one with the student. The little brothers and sisters are always welcome guests at the team's games and practices. The older athletes can model work habits, focus, unselfishness, and discipline to their younger partners.

Tradition #73—First Practice Under the Lights of the Community

❑ *Lessons from this tradition*: Fun. Unity to begin the season. Connect with the community.

People from the community position their cars circling the field. Have your team take the field in complete darkness. As soon as the players reach the center of the field, all of the drivers of the cars turn on their lights and honk their horns (on signal). The lights from the cars indicate that this team is in the spotlight of the community, not just the center of attention for representing the town, but also under scrutiny for the players' behavior. The noise created by the horns is a signal of support for the team by the community. After a few minutes, the people from the community get out of their cars and physically surround the team to demonstrate support for them and for the upcoming season.

Tradition #74—Community Leaders in the Locker Room

❑ *Lessons from this tradition*: The team is a reflection of the community. One of the lessons for the community leader is to see how much effort goes into being a good team and representing the community.

Take the time to call and schedule a variety of community leaders to address your team during the season. Leaders can speak on leadership, the importance of the team to the community, their personal experiences, or the history of the school. On one hand, these leaders bring some credibility and a different focus to your team, and you do the same for them. Supporting the teams and schools should not just involve the parents and classmates; rather it needs to be a community-wide effort. It may be wise to establish a time limit of 5-8 minutes for a particular presentation, since most non-coaches don't understand the time constraints of practice.

11

Post-season Traditions

Tradition #75—Banquet Traditions

❏ *Lessons from this tradition*: Demonstrating thanks to everyone who has helped you along the way.

• Invite every coach to attend the season-ending banquet who has worked with the seniors at any time during their career. Have each senior acknowledge the impact that the individuals have had on his life. It is amazing to see a senior with the person who coached him when he was much younger.

• Recognize and reward players who have played other sports to encourage multi-sport participation.

• Have each player and coach write something about each player and combine everyone's comments and use them to introduce each player at the banquet.

• Have one player introduce another. Underclassmen can introduce a senior; they can choose whom they would like to introduce or the coach can assign the player. Before the banquet, each player needs to check with the coach so he can screen and add input (if necessary) to what is being said.

Tradition #76—Scrapbook From the Year

❏ *Lessons from this tradition*: Creating visible memories.

Get a parent volunteer to collect every newspaper article and picture from the season, make copies of the collected materials, and turn them into a season scrapbook for each of the players. Seniors scrapbooks can contain items of value to the senior, such as a letter from each of his teammates and coaches, a combined summary of things written about him by his teammates, etc.

Tradition #77—Reward Your Core Covenants

❏ *Lessons from this tradition*: Our values have value.

Think about the awards you give at the end of the season. Do they reflect what you believe? Do they reward the things your program stands for? If you emphasize a "team-first attitude" all year long and then give an "MVP" trophy at the end of the season, does such an award match up with your words? A trophy for Most Valuable Player rewards individual skill, individual statistics, and individual play. If you truly believe in a "team-first" attitude, your awards should reflect that. The award should be an MVT (Most Valuable Teammate). If you are trying to develop determination in your players, give out a DIMITT award (Determination Is More Important Than Talent). Reward the things described in your Core Covenants (Character, Work Habits, Enthusiasm, and Team First)

Tradition #78—Assess the Season with Seniors

❏ *Lessons from this tradition*: Buy in with the program. Shaping the future of the program. Investing in the team tradition.

Take the time to meet with the graduating seniors individually after the season has concluded. Allow them to have the freedom to open up and be truthful, without becoming defensive. Encourage feedback. Allow the seniors to identify the problems and the names of problem teammates. The strengths of the program will be easy for them to talk about and are equally important, but if your team is going to grow, listen to the people who were in the inner circle. Write down all suggestions that will potentially make your program better.

12

Alumni Traditions

Tradition #79—Send Program Information

❑ *Lessons from this tradition*: The team wants you to remain part of the program. You will forever be appreciated and be a part of the team's history.

Take the time every year to update your alumni address book. Send every former player, information on the season and players at the beginning of the season. Email attachments will save time and money. Include schedules, bios, records, coach's comments and a reminder that they are always welcome in the locker room.

Tradition #80—Adopt a Player

❑ *Lessons from this tradition*: You still are part of the program. A few current athletes may need some assistance with the costs of summer programs or equipment.

Invite former players to "adopt" a player on your current team who may need some financial assistance, or a summer job to be able to afford shoes, some other essential piece of equipment, camp attendance, etc.

Tradition #81—Summer Nights Connections

❑ *Lessons from this tradition*: Connection with the past. Help for current players to prepare for the season.

During the summer, schedule an alumni game and then a dinner, where past players talk about what they learned and/or remember from their high-school experiences. Match up current players with some of the graduates.

Tradition #82—Bring Them All Back

❑ *Lessons from this tradition*: Connect the past with the present. Honor past players. Keep history alive.

Choose one night every four or five years and bring back every team for alumni night. For the teams that are healthy enough, play an alumni tournament. Attempt to contact and bring back every ex-coach.

Tradition #83—Personal Note to Alumni *
(*Submitted by Coach Greg Oldham, head girl's basketball coach; Coupeville High School, Coupeville, WA)

❑ *Lessons from this tradition*: Players making a personal connection with the history of the program. You are part of our current program.

We take time during one practice to write alumni from our program. Kids who have a personal connection to a graduate write notes, and I send these and any cool handouts/posters/ sayings to the former players to help keep them connected to our program. We also often have former players give a short pre-game or post-game talk. I've also had former opponents do the same.

Tradition #84—Birthdays

❑ *Lessons from this tradition*: You care about your players.

Birthdays are a special day for most people. As such, if a coach can keep at list of players' birthdays, it doesn't take much effort to make a call and let them know you are thinking about them. Great kids stay in your life, and caring coaches make the effort to show the players that they still care.

Tradition #85—Numbers Have a Special Meaning

❑ *Lessons from this tradition*: Connection to the past through your game number. Know your history.

Every athlete remembers their game number. As a method of tracking your number, keep a list of every player who has ever worn each of the numbers. Send a card with the list of all the players, past and present, who have worn the number. Players wearing a number for the first time need to memorize all of the former players who have worn their number.

13

Academic Traditions

Tradition #86—Steak, Hamburgers or Beans

❑ *Lessons from this tradition*: Get to work on your grades. Academic motivation. Humor.

When the first quarter grades come out, have a barbecue at the coach's house. The player's menu is dependant on their first quarter GPA. If they achieved a GPA higher than a 3.2, they eat steak. If their GPA is between 2.2 and 3.2, they eat hamburgers. If their GPA is under 2.2, they eat beans. Make allowances for high effort but low achievement. This academic dinner can also be done on the first road trip of the season.

Tradition #87—On A Roll

❑ *Lessons from this tradition*: Support, encouragement and reward for athletes who are making improvement in their academic performance.

Too often, the only recognition given to athletes for academic performance is when they have reached an accepted level of success (e.g., honor roll, dean's list, etc.). One of the rules of motivation is that if you want people to change, you must recognize and support any positive changes they make along the way. If you wait for them to reach the summit before rewarding them, too many won't make it. By rewarding positive change, no matter how small, people are more motivated to continue to grow. Identify student athletes who may be struggling in your program, and then, on a weekly basis, give them special notice if their teachers say they have shown improved effort or results during the week. You are supporting the teachers' effort to have your athlete succeed in their classes, and you are publicly praising the athlete every step along the way. Call the endeavor "on a roll." They don't have to be on the honor roll to be on a roll.

Tradition #88—Letter to the Faculty

❑ *Lessons from this tradition*: Connecting with the academic portion of the school.

Take the time to compose and send a letter to the faculty at the beginning of the season that addresses your program. Discuss the academic, athletic, and behavioral expectations. Let the faculty know that they are an important part of the player's lives (as are athletics) and that it is essential that they and you work together to assist each of the students you share. Give the faculty members the information they need to get hold of you to be proactive with any problems. Send a schedule of practices and games with an open invitation to observe "your classroom".

Tradition #89—Academic Coach

❑ *Lessons from this tradition*: Connection with and support of the academic department of your school.

Assign one assistant coach to each academic area to check with the players' teachers on all players' efforts and behavior, as well as accomplishments. Let the teachers know that you are working with them and in support of them to help the athlete give their best effort in their classroom. Bring your program to them. Keep the dialogue open and let the teachers know everyone is after the same goals for the players. This "academic assistant" can also invite the teachers to come to practice and games, so that they can see the students succeed in a different arena and also to make a connection with their students outside of the classroom. This effort can help enhance the relationship between the teachers and the students and level of success achieved by the students.

Tradition #90—Academic Patches

❑ *Lessons from this tradition*: Identifying academic achievement. Rewarding academic success in a manner similar to what you use to distinguish athletic success.

Look at how you currently publicly recognize athletic success (e.g., decals, locker stickers, pins for wrestling, success dots, etc.) and provide the same thing for academic success and or extra effort. They could also be academic patches that are worn on their uniforms, similar to captain's patches.

Tradition #91—Most Respected Teacher

❑ *Lessons from this tradition*: The people who are working with the players in the classroom are respected.

Sometime during the season, have each player name the current teacher whom they most respect. Coaches can then send a note saying that one or more of the players have selected them for this honor. Then, those teachers can be invited to come watch a practice or part of a practice (your classroom). This effort creates a win-win situation for the athlete and teacher, connecting them in a positive way. Often times, teachers who are not coaches and were not athletes have no idea what it takes to be on a team. Players learn that they need to look at teachers more respectfully, while teachers make a positive connection with the program. Because teachers are seldom given enough positive feedback for the work that they do, this tradition helps to address that shortcoming by sincerely demonstrating to them that they are respected for what they are doing.

14

Equipment Traditions

Tradition #92—Locker of Champions

❏ *Lessons from this tradition*: The team's heritage is important. Connect with former players. Take care of the facilities and equipment. Tying the past with the present everyday when the athlete opens his locker. Daily reminder of past successes and the tradition of excellence.

If you have an "athletic locker room" or a team room, take the time to place the names of every player who was part of a championship team in their particular locker. The name goes in the exact locker the player was using during that season and stays in the locker with new names being added on every time a championship is won. Get a coach with great handwriting to do every name, so that the names are all the same size and style. Use a permanent pen (and great handwriting), or a plaque, to list the former champions' names on or in their locker. The information that should be listed includes the player's name, the player's game number, the player's sport (e.g., FB, BB, BA, SB, WR. VB, etc.), and the year the championship was won. (For example, Ben Windham - #80–FB–'96) Athletes should use the same locker if they play multiple sports so that their name can reflect every team and year they played on a championship team. After a few years, the list of names becomes part of the history of the program, the locker room, and the person. When players choose their locker, they are sharing it with a past champion or big brother or sister.

New players will often choose their locker for the year by looking in to see who they are sharing with from history. Former players will return to the locker room years later to see if their name is still there and who has joined them on the list of championships.

Tradition #93—Game Numbers

❑ *Lessons from this tradition*: Academics are emphasized in our program.

Almost every player has a certain number they want for their game uniform. This tradition offers a clear-cut method for prioritizing distribution of the uniform numbers. The player with the highest GPA (from the last quarter, semester or overall) is given first choice of numbers and then the process continues in descending order. If two player have the same GPA, the honor goes to the player who has made the most improvement since the last grading period. This tradition can also be done by grade level.

Tradition #94—One Program K-12*
(*Submitted by Beth Campbell, head girl's basketball coach;
Bellevue Christian High School, Bellevue, WA)

❑ *Lessons from this tradition*: Unity throughout the program. Tying every player to the program—from the youngest to the seniors. Big sisters—little sisters. Identify with the team

After a T-shirt with your team slogan or theme for the year has been designed, instead of having a special "varsity only," warm-up shirt, provide the same shirt for the whole program—K-12. This way, every young athlete in the city who attends your summer camp can wear the same warm-up shirt as the varsity does during their pre-game warm ups. Varsity players who share the same number with their younger counterparts can have their own connection.

15

Facilities Traditions

Tradition #95—Walk of Fame

❏ *Lessons from this tradition*: Tying the past to the present. Honoring people who have helped build the program.

Honor the people who have meant the most to your program by building a walkway to the field with steppingstones engraved with their names. It can be an honor bestowed on former players, donors, supporters, past coaches, or championship teams.

Tradition #96—Paw Prints

❏ *Lessons from this tradition*: Building on past successes. Daily reminder. Most battles are won before they are fought.

Paint an insignia that represents your mascot (e.g., paw prints) on the ground leading to the weight room (championships are won in the weight room). Inside every insignia, place a championship year.

Tradition #97—Dummy Adoption

❏ *Lessons from this tradition*: Seniors have the most invested. Even the most trivial jobs can be made important and fun.

Have each of your seniors "adopt" some piece of equipment and be responsible for it everyday. For example, senior football linemen can adopt a specific blocking dummy. They make sure that it gets to and from the field every day. They need to have a back-up baby sitter in case they are not at practice. They can name their dummy (e.g., teachers, principal, sister, brother, movie star, girl/boy friend, cartoon character etc.), and they can place a temporary, personal identification mark on the dummy. They can also be responsible for passing along the "tradition of the dummy" to the next generation of linemen, or the honor can be awarded by a coach for a player who earned it for a specific accomplishment (e.g., the quality of a player's weight-room effort during the summer).

Tradition #98—Carry Equipment for Others

❏ *Lessons from this tradition*: Helping teammates. Seeing things from a different perspective.

Have your players be responsible for the care of the equipment that they use the least in order to honor their teammates who have different roles. For example, the quarterbacks and offensive backs have responsibility for the blocking sled. The defensive backs can care for the blocking dummies. The offensive linemen (who are typically among the biggest and strongest players on the team) have responsibility for the scrimmage vests, while the linebackers and/or defensive linemen are accountable for the practice balls.

16

Traditions with Weekly Themes and Slogans

Tradition #99—Character Traits as Themes of the Week*

❑ *Lessons from this tradition*: Athletes are expected to learn and become people of character. Connection with different parts of your community. Lessons of character abound everywhere.

Sports are often given credit for teaching life skills. Does this teaching automatically occur by someone merely being close to or involved in the action? Although it may be true for some athletes, coaches cannot make the assumption that simply being part of an athletic experience will ensure that the participants will learn the essential lessons of life. Like anything else coaches hope to accomplish in their sport, *they must plan for it, and teach it if they want it to happen*. Coaches should not leave the opportunity to develop young men and women of character to chance.

One of the best methods for coaches to ensure the essential life lessons are learned is to identify what their particular sport is capable of teaching the participants, and then to take the time to focus on each aspect as a *theme of the day or week*. Such an effort will require some time and planning by the coaching staff to prepare for these presentations just as they do for any other part of their practice.

Planning

Before the season begins, one of the tasks of the coaching staff is to identify which lessons they want to focus on during the year and then schedule these lessons in to the practice calendar. Each day, coaches should plan a few minutes into the beginning and/or end of every practice to have a presentation that emphasizes the theme for the week. It will require some research and thought to make it meaningful to their team.

---

*Based on material in the book, *1001 Motivational Messages—Teaching Character Through Sport*, by Bruce Brown; Monterey, CA: Coaches Choice; 2001. Among the themes which are covered in this book are the following: work habits, enthusiasm, courage, integrity, perseverance, winning and losing, discipline, great competitors, confidence, poise, sportsmanship, friendship, and teamwork.

After the coaching staff has decided on the themes for the season, it may benefit you to fit them on to their game calendar. Although the main focus of a coaching staff is on their own athletes, some themes may be more appropriately scheduled based on the team's opponent. For example, in a week, the team is going to play a team that has a history of unsportsmanlike behavior, the chosen theme may be poise. That way, the coaches are keeping their focus on their preparation and the nees to demonstrate poise so their opponent's choices do not draw their players into poor behavior or penalties.

One coach can take the responsibility for the themes in order to schedule presenters, do bulletin boards, player letters, etc., but all coaches need to participate in the presenting, teaching, correcting and modeling of the themes.

Presenters

Presenters have proven to be more effective when they are allowed to volunteer and also to choose which theme they want to present. A variety of presenters can be employed with equal success.

• Coaches: Coaches need to be part of every presentation. Whether it is introducing the speaker or the theme, following up with reminders during or at the end of practice, or making the presentation, coaches are an essential ingredient of the process. Often times, coaches will conclude practice with a reminder and a chance for athletes to talk briefly on what they have learned about the theme and how it applies to the sport or their life outside sport. When a team is first beginning to incorporate this tradition into their practices, it may be easier to do these follow-ups in smaller groups especially if it is a larger team activity (e.g., track, football). The head coach needs to continue to pull the themes together throughout the season.

• Athletes: Once themes have been established as a tradition in the program, athletes will often quickly volunteer for an opportunity to present a particular theme (sometimes a year ahead of time). But when this program is just beginning, the athletes may be reluctant to get involved. Coaches should encourage their team leaders to take a theme and allow the players to go over it with them before they present the theme. The athletes should always be able to respond to the presentation with questions or thoughts of their own.

Times will occur when specific athletes are asked to present certain themes in order to help them make behavioral changes. For example, an athlete who may be struggling with sportsmanship or poise can greatly benefit from preparing and addressing those particular topics in front of his team and coaches.

• Staff: Having an administrator, faculty or staff member present once during the week is a great way to build a relationship between the team and the school. It also gives that person some insight and appreciation for what the coaches are trying to do for the athlete's lives outside of the sport and winning games. It is surprising how flattered people are to be asked by an athlete or coach to address the team. For example, athletes could be asked to nominate the teachers whom they would like to have speak. Players and coaches are always encouraged to ask questions or make comments from their perspective that will assist in the understanding of the theme. After a staff member has made this connection with the team, both an improved relationship between the student/athlete and the staff and an increased attendance at games by those from "the outside" who have been asked to be involved in this effort often occur.

• Community Members: Having members of the community present during these theme-sharing sessions can be very beneficial. Every community usually has a wealth of talent from which to draw. Religious leaders, ex-athletes, people who have overcome adversity, community leaders, and parents, can all serve as effective presenters. One of the steps that can be undertaken to form a historical connection with the program is to have former athletes come back and present to the current players. Establishing any kind of positive tradition always gives a person's athletic experience additional value and the program a more meaningful history. This tradition can be particularly effective before a "big game" or playoff.

Tradition #100—CHAMPS or CHAMPIONS or KNIGHTS

❏ *Lessons from this tradition*: Tying the team's mascot or school to positive team-building or character-building themes.

Use words from your program to build acronyms with a character base. Any single word can be used to turn your goal or your nickname into a positive, powerful and memorable acronym.

> Example: Bobcats
>
> **B** = brave
>
> **O** = optimistic
>
> **B** = brothers
>
> **C** = confidence
>
> **A** = attitude
>
> **T** = teamwork
>
> **S** = sportsmanship

The following words can be drawn from the alphabet to build acronyms for your team.

A attitude, action, accomplishment, ambition

B brothers, beginnings, blessings, brave

C challenges, communication, compete, confidence, courage, coachable, commitment, character

D determination, discipline, diligence, dignity, dreams, duty, dependable

E enthusiasm, enjoyment, ethical, encouragement, effort

F friendship, fairness, faith, family

G generosity, grace, greatness

H habits, hard work, honor, heart, heroes, hope, humor, honesty, humility, have fun

I integrity, ideals, imagination, improvement

J joy, justice

K knowledge, kindness, kindred

L loyalty, leadership, laughter, love

M motivated, memories, modesty, mentally tough

N nobilit

O one heart beat, oath, optimism

P poise, preparation, passion, praise, promises, perseverance

Q quality

R respect, responsibility, reliability

S sincerity, service, standards higher than victory, self discipline, strength, selflessness, sportsmanship

T team work, team first, thankfulness, truth, teachable spirit

U unselfishness, unity, understanding

V valor, victory

W warrior, wishes, work hard, work habits

X xciting, xtra effort

Y youcancountonme, ynot?,

Z zeal

Tradition #101—Positive Athletic Slogans

❑ *Lessons from this tradition*: Fun. Unity slogan.

Use positive athletic slogans to promote your team's Core Covenants and to represent your team on T-shirts, banners or themes. The following 101 slogans can be used in that regard.

1. Tradition Never Graduates
2. The Spirit of Past Warriors Goes Before Us—Hanta Yo
3. Are you in or are you out?
4. Precision Performance
5. Work, Play, Win Together
6. State of Determination
7. REPS - Repetition Elevates Personal Skills
8. Getting down to business (basics)
9. Smashville—baseball—softball
10. NEC—No Excuses for Champions
11. Attitudes are Contagious—Is Yours Worth Catching?
12. Hungry for More—Back for More
13. Unleashed (mascot: dogs—cats—bulls, etc.)
14. Tradition is Ours
15. Building Tradition, Together—Team
16. The Next Level
17. Becoming the Best—Becoming a Team
18. In the Game
19. The Power of the Dream
20. I'm a Believer—We are Believers
21. 639 Miles to *State*
22. Bird Mascots—Fly Somewhere New
23. Taking the State by Storm (Wave—Bark— Roar)—Mascot Storm, Hurricanes, etc.
24. The Perfect Storm
25. Paint the Town *Purple* (school color)

26. Welcome to *Hoops* City

27. Don't get Bit – Dogs

28. Join the *Green* (school color) Team

29. One Team – One Goal

30. It's all about WE

31. From the advertisement Got Milk. *Got Blue*? (school color); Got Snacks? (linemen); Got Biscuits? (mascot - dogs); Got Team? (Tigers, Trojans, Bears, etc.); Got Mice? (mascot - cats)

32. See You Under the Lights (wrestling, football, soccer, baseball, softball)

33. Building Character, Tradition and Excellence

34. It's No Secret, These Guys (Gals) Can Play

35. Warriors, Legends, Legacies, *Kings* (mascot)

36. More than a Game

37. Come Along for the Ride

38. B mascot or color black—Badgers in Black

39. Leaving it all on the floor—lay it on the line

40. It is Easy Being Green—school color green

41. Tradition, Pride and Dedication

42. Anyone, Anytime, Anywhere

43. Take Me Out to the Ball Game

44. Team First Volunteer

44. You Can't Teach Heart

45. Stay to Play Another Day

46. Good choices lead to good seasons

47. If it is to be, it is up to me

48. DIMITT—determination is more important than talent

49. Stand around somewhere else—we are here to work

50. Game Day

51. Work Today—Play Tomorrow

52. Attitude is a Choice—Attitude is a Decision—Attitude is a Habit

54. High Expectations—High Standards

55. Nothing Will Work Unless We Do

56. Blackout Friday—school color is black

57. Born to Run (basketball, track, XC, baseball, softball, football)

58. Born to Fly (passing team, fast team)

59. Together Everyone Achieves More—TEAM

60. "Get to's"* (*Submitted by Greg Oldham, head girl's basketball coach; Coupeville High School, Coupeville, WA). No one in our program is allowed to say "have to." We don't believe in "have to's"; everything we do is a "get to." That's made a big change in how we perceive hard work.

61. Unity Begins With You

62. On Any Given Night

63. Tribe—"A band of people who shared a common history, acknowledged a common authority, faced a common danger, and expected a common future. They all agreed on what work needed to be done and who was the enemy."

64. WIN—What is Important Now? A reminder to quickly recover from mistakes and setbacks. Teammates can use this acronym to remind each other to get back to complete concentration, be ready for the next play and that they are supported.

65. Next play—forget what just happened (good or bad) and get on with the next play

66. WIT—Whatever It Takes. However much work is required, we are committed

67. Small town—Big tradition (Submitted by Mark Perry, head football coach; Snohomish High School, Snohomish, WA)

68. Here Come the Irish (mascot)

69. Responsible for Continuing the Tradition—reminder to players of the past successes of the program

70. It is the players, not the plays, who win games

71. Enthusiasm makes our muscles stronger, our feet faster and our hearts unite (BOH—Become One Heartbeat)

72. Live it or be quiet—act in a way that your beliefs (Core Covenants) are seen and do not need to be told to people.

73. LUCK—Living Under Christ's Kingdome

74. It is not the potential, it is the performance

75. Decrease Me—Increase Us

76. NBT/NBP—No Better Time, No Better Place

77. Seize the Season

78. Be positive, enjoy yourself and make it fun for everyone

79. Back to Basics

80. Without the burn, you will never learn

81. An athlete delivers on their word

82. Morale is to physical as four is to one

83. Old School—Be Strong In Body, Clean In Mind and Lofty In Ideals (Quote by Dr. James Naismith)

84. Big dreams create magic

85. Hard work leads to success; more success leads to inner confidence; confidence leads to more success—everything starts with work—ESWW

86. Turn it around, today

87. Benjamin Disraeli: "The secret of success in constancy of purpose"—shared purpose

88. Don't get by, get better

89. Get better today – improve every day

90. NGU—Never Give Up

91. A Winner Makes Commitments

92. Accept the Challenge

93. Decrease my light, increase our light

94. I will give out before I give up

95. Believe in the Power of We

96. ESWM – enthusiasm starts with me

97. SYOE – start your own engine

98. Be great in the small things—Be great in critical situations

99. Excellence without arrogance

100. Greatness is achieved through the discipline of attending to detail

101. The Pride and Tradition of the ___(mascot)__ will be entrusted to the Courageous, Committed and Strong

Call for Contributions

Open Letter to Coaches

Dear Coach,

Volume II of *Positive Athletic Traditions* is currently being written. If you have any positive athletic traditions that you would like to share, please send them to: Bruce E Brown – bbrown8164@aol.com. If your tradition is used in the next volume of *Positive Athletic Traditions*, you and your program will be given credit for the tradition that you submitted, and you will be sent a free copy of the second edition.

Sincerely,

Bruce Eamon Brown

About the Author

Bruce Eamon Brown is a special presenter for the NAIA's "Champions of Character Program." Previously, he served as the athletic director at Northwest College in Kirkland, Washington. A retired coach, he worked at every level of education in his more than three decades of teaching and coaching. His coaching experiences included basketball, football, volleyball, and baseball at the junior high and high school levels, and basketball at the junior college and college levels. He was involved with championship teams at each level of competition.

Brown is a much sought-after speaker, who frequently addresses coaches, players, and parents on selected aspects concerning participation in sport. He has written several books, including the highly acclaimed *1001 Motivational Messages and Quotes: Teaching Character Through Sport* and *Another 1001 Motivational Messages and Quotes: Featuring the 7 Essentials of Great Teams*. He has also been the featured speaker on several well-received instructional videos:

- *Basketball Skills and Drills for Younger Players: Volume 7 – Individual Defense*
- *Basketball Skills and Drills for Younger Players: Volume 8 – Team Defense*
- *Basketball Skills and Drills for Younger Players: Volume 9 – Fast Break*
- *Basketball Skills and Drills for Younger Players: Volume 10 – Zone Offense*
- *Basketball Skills and Drills for Younger Players: Volume 11 – The Role of Parents in Athletics*
- *Basketball Skills and Drills for Younger Players: Volume 12 – Motivating Your Athletes*
- *Fun Ways to End Basketball Practice*
- *Team Building Through Positive Conditioning*
- *Redefining the Term "Athlete" – Using the Five Core Values*
- *How to Teach Character Through Sport*
- *The Role of Parents in Athletics*
- *Basic 8 Defensive Drill*

Brown and his wife, Dana, have five daughters, Allison, Katie, Shannon, Bridget, and Dana. The family resides in Camano Island, Washington.